IMAGES OF WAR

# THE INVASION OF SICILY 1943

## RARE PHOTOGRAPHS FROM WARTIME ARCHIVES

Jon Diamond



Pen & Sword
MILITARY

First published in Great Britain in 2017 by
**PEN & SWORD MILITARY**
An imprint of
Pen & Sword Books Ltd
47 Church Street
Barnsley
South Yorkshire
S70 2AS



ISBN 978-1-47389-609-3



A CIP catalogue record for this book is available from the British Library.



Typeset by Concept, Huddersfield, West Yorkshire HD4 5JL.
Printed and bound in England by CPI Group (UK) Ltd, Croydon CR0 4YY.

Pen & Sword Books Ltd incorporates the imprints of Pen & Sword Archaeology, Atlas, Aviation, Battleground, Discovery, Family History, History, Maritime, Military, Naval, Politics, Railways, Select, Social History, Transport, True Crime, and Claymore Press, Frontline Books, Leo Cooper, Praetorian Press, Remember When, Seaforth Publishing and Wharncliffe.

For a complete list of Pen & Sword titles please contact
PEN & SWORD BOOKS LIMITED
47 Church Street, Barnsley, South Yorkshire S70 2AS, England
E-mail: enquiries@pen-and-sword.co.uk
Website: www.pen-and-sword.co.uk

# Contents

**Acknowledgements** . . . . . . . . . . . . . . . . . . . . . . . . . . . . . . 4

Chapter One
**Strategic Prelude to the Invasion of Sicily** . . . . . . . . . . . 5

Chapter Two
**Terrain, Fortifications and Installations** . . . . . . . . . . . 44

Chapter Three
**Commanders and Combatants** . . . . . . . . . . . . . . . . . . . . 118

Chapter Four
**The Landings and Axis Counter-attacks** . . . . . . . . . . . . . 160

Chapter Five
**Allied Advances and Sicilian Objectives Captured** . . . . . 212

**Epilogue** . . . . . . . . . . . . . . . . . . . . . . . . . . . . . . . . . . 237

**Bibliography** . . . . . . . . . . . . . . . . . . . . . . . . . . . . . . . 248

# Acknowledgements

This archival photograph volume in the *Images of War* series is dedicated to the men and women who fought and perished during the thirty-eight-day campaign to wrest Sicily from Axis control in the summer of 1943. We ponder upon viewing the photographs to remind us of their heroic sacrifice to maintain freedom lest we forget. The author also wishes to acknowledge the many military history scholars including such names as Blumenson, D'Este, Garland, Smyth, Porch, Whiting, Zaloga and Atkinson, to name but a few, who have catalogued the nuances of this campaign with their superlative prose. The author is indebted to the able assistance of the archivists at both the United States Army Military History Institute (USAMHI) at the United States Army War College in Carlisle, Pennsylvania and the Still Photo Section of the National Archives and Records Administration (NARA) in College Park, Maryland.

## Chapter One

# Strategic Prelude to the Invasion of Sicily

The first official summit held between neutral America's President Franklin D. Roosevelt and British Prime Minister Winston S. Churchill occurred during the Atlantic Conference in Placentia Bay, Canada on 8–9 August 1941. It would be another five months before the entry of the United States into the war, which followed Imperial Japan's aerial attack on Pearl Harbor and invasion of the Philippine Archipelago. At that meeting in Newfoundland, Canada, nascent plans to better co-ordinate allocation of American war *matériel* and foodstuffs, through Lend-Lease, were reinforced. Both Britain and the Soviet Union, the latter invaded by Germany on 22 June 1941, were desperately attempting to contain the ceaseless expansion of Adolf Hitler and Benito Mussolini's Axis forces in North Africa and across Russia in order to protect the many strategic locales, such as the Suez Canal, the Caucasus and Middle Eastern oilfields, and Moscow. Also, at this Placentia Bay Conference in Canada, the Atlantic Charter was crafted that outlined the goals of the Allies for after defeating the Axis belligerents.

After the entry of the United States into the global conflict, the Combined Chiefs of Staff (CCS), a body comprising both American and British service chiefs and their principal aides, was formalised at the Arcadia Conference in Washington from 22 December to 14 January 1941. At this initial Washington Conference, the Allies decided that their major effort was to be directed towards Europe to ultimately bring about the defeat of Germany. Also, the Allied nations would not make any separate peace with the enemy. Even before Pearl Harbor, Roosevelt and Churchill considered the Nazi regime as a more dangerous threat to their countries and survival, and they had adopted a strategy to vanquish the Axis partners of Germany and Italy first. In Asia and the Pacific, primarily defensive or limited actions were to be conducted against the Japanese until European victory was secure. The ill-fated and short-lived American-British-Dutch-Australian (ABDA) command for the Far East, under British General Archibald Wavell, was also established at the Arcadia Conference. However, it was dissolved by mid-February 1942, following the ignoble defeats suffered by Allied forces at Singapore and throughout the Dutch East Indies at the hands of Imperial Japan.

The Japanese juggernaut of 1941–1942 over the Allies in the Far East and the Pacific established hegemony over a new Tokyo-controlled Greater East Asia Co-Prosperity Sphere. This enormous geographical area included a vast swathe of China along with total domination of Burma, Malaya and Singapore, the Dutch East Indies, the Philippine and Bismarck Archipelagos, and almost all of the Solomon Islands. Advanced Japanese bases along Papua New Guinea's northern coast at Buna and Gona, as well as at Lae in North-east New Guinea's Huon Peninsula, were established for Imperial Japanese Army (IJA) and Navy (IJN) offensive action against Port Moresby, which lay across the Arafura Sea from Australia's Northern Territory. Australia's northernmost principal port, Darwin, had been bombed by the Japanese from February 1942. A planned Japanese south-eastern thrust into the New Hebrides, Fiji and Tonga island groups, if accomplished, would have created havoc by severing American sea lanes to the Antipodes, thereby denying the Allies a strategically-important geographic springboard for future offensive operations.

The interval from October 1942 to January 1943 has been referred to as a 'turning of the tide' in the epic struggle of the Second World War. During this three-month time-frame five major land campaigns were conducted leading to staggering losses for the Axis partners of Germany and Italy as well as for Imperial Japan, at the expense of a very attenuated Allied war production machine to meet the global confrontation requirements. These included the protracted battles by American and Australian formations for Papua, New Guinea; Guadalcanal, in the southern Solomon Islands of the South Pacific area; the defence of Stalingrad, resulting in the surrender of large numbers of Axis coalition troops, comprising mostly the *Wehrmacht* Sixth Army; the 'see-saw' British and Dominion forces' operations, first confronting the eastwardly-advancing Italian Tenth Army; and then against General Erwin Rommel's *Deutsches Afrika Korps*, combined with the remnants of Mussolini's North African expeditionary force, across the Western Desert encompassing Egypt and the Cyrenaican portion of Libya. These chaotic internecine engagements, employing both large mechanised forces as well as defensive lines, would initially culminate in the First and Second Battles of El Alamein in July and October 1942, respectively, and then the Anglo-American invasion of Vichy French-controlled Morocco and Algeria in north-west Africa on 8 November 1942, Operation *Torch.* A gruelling six-month campaign for control of Tunisia would ensue until May 1943.

At Guadalcanal in the Southern Solomon Islands, throughout a hellacious jungle and gruesome naval surface campaign from 7 August 1942 to 9 February 1943, the heroic defence by, initially, the 1st Marine Division (Reinforced) followed by regimental elements of the US Army's Americal Division enabled the Americans to maintain possession of Henderson Field as an 'unsinkable aircraft carrier'. Coupled with the gallant sacrifices of Allied seamen and American pilots, IJN Combined Fleet Admiral Isoruku Yamamoto and IJA Lieutenant-General Harukichi Hyakutake's naval bombardment and island counter-attacks, respectively, failed to re-capture Guadalcanal, thereby deterring the potentially nightmarish maritime scenario of Japanese naval expansion into the South-eastern Pacific Ocean with potential severance of the sea lanes connecting the United States and Australia and New Zealand.

Coincident with the struggle for Guadalcanal, Australian Militia battalions, reinforced later by Australian Imperial Defence Force (AIF) veterans returning from the Middle East, stopped a Japanese amphibious invasion at Milne Bay at Papua's eastern tip from 25 August to 6 September 1942. Also, an enemy over-land attack across the Owen Stanley Mountains via the Kokoda Trail stalled in mid-September 1942, a mere 27 air miles from the Australian-American main staging area at Port Moresby. After those Japanese setbacks, both American and Australian forces, going onto the offensive, would be severely bloodied in their attempts to re-capture the northern Papuan Japanese entrenched garrisons at Buna and Gona from October 1942 to January 1943. These actions were to herald the fanatical defence that the Japanese were to mount throughout the Pacific War.

Ultimately, the costly Allied victories along Papua's northern coast and on Guadalcanal would usher in the counter-offensives against the recently acquired Japanese bastions by General Douglas A. MacArthur's South-west Pacific Area (SWPA) forces westward across New Guinea and Vice Admiral William F. Halsey's South Pacific Force up the Solomon Island chain. Both campaigns conducted simultaneously would keep the IJA and IJN strategically off balance. Acquisition of existing and construction of new airfields in both zones would enable the aerial neutralisation of Rabaul on New Britain Island in the Bismarck Archipelago during Operation *Cartwheel*, making an amphibious bloodbath there unnecessary.

By October 1942, two Nazi armies had driven forward deep into the Soviet interior's Caucasus Mountains but had become bogged some way from the Baku oil fields that Hitler desperately sought to fuel his war effort. Just to the north of the Caucasus Mountains was the city of Stalingrad on the Volga River. At that eponymous locale, Soviet forces conducted an epic defence within that city's ruins against *Wehrmacht* General Friedrich Paulus and his vaunted Sixth Army, some of Hitler's finest troops. On 2 October, Paulus unleashed his last offensive against the Russians in Stalingrad, namely a 2,000-yard deep pocket, which included the gutted remains of buildings and factories. It was to become the farthest point that the German Sixth and Fourth Panzer Armies would advance to. The German gains were measured in yards and Paulus admitted to his peers, 'Things are going very slowly, but every day we make a little progress. The whole thing is a question of time and manpower.' The *Wehrmacht* could not do anything to delay winter's onset nor could they tap into any ready reinforcements for Paulus' dwindling Sixth Army ranks. The German High Command knew that if Stalingrad were not captured within a month, the whole Nazi position in southern Russia would be a precarious one since their flanks to the north and west were held by Rumanian troops. As would happen, the flanks were overrun by a Russian winter counter-offensive and, despite General von Manstein's attempt to open a corridor to Paulus' troops, the Sixth Army was encircled and forced to surrender. The loss of the Sixth Army's twenty divisions doomed the German invasion of the Soviet Union. The Allied planning for Operation *Torch*, the first Anglo-American amphibious assault, would have been for naught had the Germans won their epic clash with the Soviets on the Volga at Stalingrad.

The prelude for both Operation *Torch* and the Sicilian Campaign of July 1943 began with the combat events that transpired in Egypt's Western Desert and Libya's Cyrenaican province, from 9 December 1940 through 8 November 1942, the latter date roughly corresponding to the British Eighth Army victory at El Alamein and the Anglo-American Operation *Torch* landings in Morocco and Algeria. An ensuing bitter, contentious six-month campaign for Tunisia, following the Anglo-American armistice with Vichy, ensued between the Allies and a new Axis army formed by massive reinforcements sent to Tunis and Bizerte from southern Italy and Sicily.

The Italian fascist dictator Benito Mussolini gave the British War Cabinet its *entrée* into a land battle against the junior Axis partner across the North African littoral and in rugged and remote East Africa, rather than a dreaded campaign back on the enemy-occupied European continent or somewhere in Norway. On 11 June 1940, as the French were about to capitulate, Mussolini declared war on Britain and France. Soon thereafter, in the late summer of 1940, Italy's Tenth Army, under Marshal Rodolfo Graziani, launched its laborious advance across the frontier from the Cyrenaican third of Libya into Egypt. This would later develop into a full-scale theatre of war, which pitted British and Dominion forces against the Axis fascist partners. Initially, General Archibald Wavell, Commander-in-Chief (C-in-C), Middle East attacked the 215,000 Italians with only 36,000 of his Western Desert Force during Operation *Compass*, ably led by British Lieutenant-General Richard O'Connor, who took every advantage of the element of surprise in the 'limited raid' from 9–11 December 1940 along the line of Nibeiwa-East and West Tummar-Sidi Barrani and then extending west to the Buqbuq area. A total of 20,000 Italians surrendered and 180 artillery guns and sixty tanks were seized as thousands more streamed westward in a pell-mell fashion across the coastal road towards Italy's other port garrisons.

With the AIF 6th Division replacing the 4th Indian Division, the coastal port of Bardia was captured on 5 January 1941. An additional 38,000 Italian prisoners along with numerous coastal guns, field-guns, anti-aircraft (AA) pieces and vehicles were captured. Wavell and O'Connor now set their eyes on Benghazi, even as Churchill was already siphoning off some of XIII Corps (formerly the Western Desert Force until 1 January 1941) and Royal Air Force (RAF) elements for an inopportune expedition against the Axis partners in Greece. Tobruk was assaulted by the Australian

6th Division and fell on 22 January 1941. More than 25,000 Italian prisoners were taken, along with hundreds of field-guns. The surviving, routed Italians continued their retreat to the west of Tobruk.

After capturing Derna on 30 January 1941, O'Connor's XIII Corps pursued the Italians along the coast with the intent of destroying the entire Italian Tenth Army. The British 7th Armoured Division moved swiftly across the desert to the south-west and cut the road below Benghazi, trapping the retreating Italians at Beda Fomm on 5 February 1941. An additional 20,000 Italians were captured along with more than 100 tanks and field-guns. Concurrently, elements of the Australian 6th Division, advancing along the coast road, captured Benghazi.

Wavell had ended any hope of O'Connor's XIII Corps being sent to Tripoli since, on 10 February, the C-in-C was instructed by the War Cabinet in London to give first and foremost priority to assisting the expeditionary force in Greece. After conquering the Cyrenaican portion of Libya and freeing the Egyptian frontier from the Italian invader, XIII Corps went onto the defensive at El Agheila at the base of the Gulf of Sirte. Tragically, the Greek venture became another British disaster, which ultimately forced an Allied evacuation from the Peloponnese and the subsequent loss of Crete to a German airborne invasion in the late spring of 1941.

In early 1941, Hitler's original plan to bolster the Italians after the defeat at Beda Fomm was to provide German anti-tank (AT), AA and armoured units, a motorised light division (5th Light) and the 15th Panzer Division. These were sent to Tripoli under the command of General Erwin Rommel, who arrived on 12 February 1941, and the nascent and vaunted *Deutsche Afrika Korps* (DAK) was soon created. Almost immediately, Rommel sent his reconnaissance units forward to bluff the British into believing he had superior strength. During the last week of March 1941, the DAK attacked and captured the British defensive position at Mersa Brega. Rommel's intent was to cut the Cyrenaican bulge, the reverse of what O'Connor had achieved only weeks before, with his initial objectives being Derna and then Tobruk. Benghazi was re-captured by the Axis on 4 April. Two days later, the 9th Australian Division withdrew from Derna into Tobruk. By 14 April, Rommel had cleared all of Cyrenaica except for the Australian units garrisoning Tobruk, who were holed up like desert rats for a historic siege. Rommel's eastward advance on Egypt was halted at Halfaya Pass, since here, Wavell re-acquired shorter lines of communication (LOC), while Rommel, without the port facilities of Tobruk, had long supply lines to the rear with limited reinforcements.

From that time point on, over a year's interval of 'see-saw' battles commenced where both the Axis versus British and Dominion forces advanced and retreated across the North African littoral in combat engagements, such as Operations *Battleaxe*, *Brevity*, and *Crusader* employing mixed arms of tanks, artillery, AT artillery, infantry 'boxes' and tactical air deployment. One reason for the series of victories and defeats each combatant side incurred during the Libyan Desert War was that armaments and personnel were diverted to other theatres of war during this fourteen-month interval from April 1941 to June 1942. German reinforcements to the North African theatre were limited due to the massive *Wehrmacht* commitment to Operation *Barbarossa* after late June 1941. Britain had sent troops and *matériel* to both the Soviet Union, its new ally, as well as overseas to the Far East as Japanese aggression intensified. After war erupted with Japan in early December 1941, Britain had a new theatre to defend and supply.

Rommel defeated first Wavell, and then, the British Eighth Army (formed in September 1941) under a variety of commanders, sending them reeling back to, first, the British advanced base at Mersa Matruh and, then, El Alamein in late June 1942 after the failed Gazala line battles. At the conclusion of the disjointed engagements along the Gazala line, Rommel promptly captured Tobruk from the 2nd South African Infantry Division on 21 June 1942 during his second investment of the port. For this Nazi victory, Hitler awarded Rommel a field marshal's baton and the German desert commander was now intent on driving straight across the Western Desert to Cairo and, perhaps, beyond.

General Claude Auchinleck, C-in-C Middle East (having replaced the dismissed Wavell in June 1941), had taken over personal command of the Eighth Army on 25 June 1942 following the Gazala defeat, with the intent of keeping this formation intact to fight again. However, Rommel smashed Auchinleck's Eighth Army defences at Mersa Matruh after a two-day running battle at the end of June 1942. Auchinleck was compelled to withdraw into a hastily-prepared series of infantry boxes along a line starting north at the coastal railway station of El Alamein and extending south to the Qattara Depression. Auchinleck's intent was to prevent the Axis seizure of Alexandria, Cairo and the Suez Canal. If Rommel could achieve those objectives in the Nile Delta, Hitler could then contemplate sending forces south from the Caucasus to link up with the now *Panzerarmee Afrika* and then assault the oil fields of Iraq and Persia.

During the First Battle of El Alamein in July 1942, where the multi-national British Eighth Army, a conglomerate of British and Dominion forces from Australia, New Zealand, South Africa, India, Sudan and Palestine, as well as expatriate soldiers from Greece, Poland and Czechoslovakia, fought valiantly, under the personal direction of Auchinleck, at locales such as Deir el Shein, Tel el Eisa, Ruweisat Ridge, Bab el Qattar, Miteirya Ridge and Tel El Mukh Khad. These Allied actions, although yielding mixed results, had the cumulative effect of stopping Rommel's *Panzerarmee Afrika* along the coastal strip north of the Quattara Depression. Nonetheless, some of the Eighth Army's senior officers, including Auchinleck, were sacked by Churchill in August 1942 and they were replaced with General Harold R.L.G. Alexander as C-in-C Middle East while command of the Eighth Army was ceded to Lieutenant-General Bernard Law Montgomery. After Churchill's original command selection, British Lieutenant-

General William H.E. 'Strafer' Gott, an old desert hand and commander of XIII Corps, met tragic circumstances. Gott, flying in from the desert to Cairo, had his plane attacked on landing at the airfield and while helping to remove wounded occupants from the plane, he was killed. His XIII Corps command went to Lieutenant-General Brian Horrocks, while XXX and X Corps were to be led by Lieutenant-General Oliver Leese and Lieutenant-General Herbert Lumsden, respectively.

Alexander was held in the utmost esteem by Churchill, as the former had presided over the last stages of the Dunkirk evacuation in June 1940 as well as the ignoble Burma retreat in the spring of 1942. During both catastrophes for British arms, Alexander had exhibited the requisite *sangfroid* of a commander as well as disengaging his defeated forces at the correct time from highly mobile enemy units. Alexander was ordered by Churchill to not preside over another British retreat but rather, 'your prime and main duty will be to take or destroy at the earliest opportunity the German-Italian Army commanded by Field Marshal Rommel together with all its supplies and establishments in Egypt and Libya.' Alexander's weapon was going to be Montgomery's re-indoctrinated and revitalised Eighth Army.

Montgomery's last battle command had been that of a division at Dunkirk, where he won the praise of the now CIGS, General Alan Brooke. Montgomery was fortunate in that his first encounter with Rommel's DAK and his Italian allies ended in a British victory at Alam Halfa in August 1942, although, some have argued that it was based on defensive strategy that Auchinleck and his staff had originated earlier. The stage was now set in the Western Desert for the last conflict that would either break the Axis alliance knocking on the doorsteps of Alexandria and Cairo or cause a horrific defeat for the British that would probably cost them the Suez Canal and, perhaps, the Middle Eastern oil fields.

The Second Battle of El Alamein would finally end the nearly two-year battle for Egypt. On 23 October 1942, Montgomery ordered the largest artillery barrage, 1,000 British guns, yet seen in the war to launch his Operation *Lightfoot*. Leese's XXX Corps attacked the northern minefields of Rommel's positions to also open a corridor for Lumsden's armour-rich X Corps. Facing Montgomery's 195,000 troops were 104,000 Axis troops, more than half of them Italians who were not as well armed as the Germans. The Eighth Army fielded more than 1,000 mostly superior tanks against fewer than 240 for the Germans and 280 obsolete models for the Italians. After almost three days of fighting, the German main defences were yet to be penetrated. Lumsden was criticised by Montgomery for not wanting to risk his tanks being too far forward of the infantry. On 26 October, the Australian 9th Division and the British 1st Armoured Division began to make some headway in the northern sector of the battle area. An enemy counter-attack on the following day was repelled by the British 1st Armoured Division's and Australians' excellent use of their 6-pounder AT guns. On 28–30 October, the 9th Australian Division continued to hammer at the northern salient aiming for the coast. As Rommel responded by shifting his armour to the north to counter the Australians, Montgomery launched Operation *Supercharge* on 1 November to the south of the Australians. The next day, a combined attack by New Zealand infantry and the 9th Armoured Brigade broke through the German defences enabling X Corps' armour to fight their way forward. From 2–4 November, a battle of attrition inevitably crumbled the Axis defences and *Panzerarmee Afrika* forces began their long retreat along the coastal road or to prisoner-of-war stockades.

Churchill stated, after Montgomery's Eighth Army victory over Rommel's vaunted *Panzerarmee Afrika* in early November 1942, that: 'Now this is not the end; it is not even the beginning of the end. But it is, perhaps, the end of the beginning.' In his monumental post-war history, Churchill wrote: 'Before Alamein we never had a victory. After Alamein, we never had a defeat.' To expand on Churchill's turn of a phrase and as the Axis forces began the long retreat from their El Alamein positions with Montgomery's Eighth Army in pursuit, the first Anglo-American offensive, Operation *Torch*, was about to be delivered as a series of major amphibious assaults at multiple locations along both the Atlantic and Mediterranean coasts of Vichy French-controlled Morocco and Algeria.

After initially rejecting a Mediterranean strategy to defeat the Axis alliance between Germany and Italy, US Army planners in Washington had proposed, in April 1942, a concentration of American forces in the United Kingdom for a full-scale attack across the English Channel into northern France in the spring of 1943. By 1942, Dwight D. Eisenhower had so impressed US Army Chief of Staff, George C. Marshall, the latter promoted him to major-general and sent him to England in the spring of 1942 to co-ordinate American planning with the British. Before the war, the largest formation that Eisenhower had commanded was an infantry battalion as a lieutenant-colonel in 1940. His meteoric rise was also aided by an appearance of affability, which underscored his commitment to fostering a cohesive Anglo-American alliance. By July 1942, he was promoted to the rank of lieutenant-general.

Churchill and his CIGS General Alan Brooke needed to engage the Axis forces somewhere. However, both feared repetition of recent continental expeditions that resulted in the fiascos at Dunkirk and Norway in the spring of 1940 and Greece in 1941. In the upcoming near future, both British leaders would also learn, in time for Operation *Torch*, that an attack on a fortified continental port was suicidal as evidenced at Dieppe during Operation *Jubilee* in August 1942, which inflicted horrific casualties on the assaulting Canadian infantry and British armour. Another failed invasion on a foreign shore might lead to the downfall to Churchill's government and impede Britain's continuation of the war. Thus, Churchill and the British planners favoured Operation *Torch*, the invasion of Morocco and Algeria, which were weakly defended by Vichy French forces and colonial troops.

Roosevelt wanted any military action in 1942 that would help Stalin's forces as the *Wehrmacht* drove deeper into Soviet Russia. Both Marshall and Eisenhower wanted no part in a Mediterranean campaign and recognised that north-west Europe would be the decisive battlefield. Ultimately, Marshall and Eisenhower were overruled and Roosevelt sided with the British on Operation *Torch* being the main campaign for 1942 in the European theatre. Roosevelt was of the opinion that American combat forces should be committed as quickly as possible in the European theatre and would not accept a plan of action that was delayed until 1943. A successful seizure of the Vichy French ports of Casablanca, Oran and Algiers, with subsequent Allied build-up and a swift move onto Tunis, would create a giant pincer against enemy forces retreating from Montgomery's Eighth Army heading westward. It was Churchill who posed Eisenhower's name for the command of Operation *Torch*, during which 'Ike' was to serve as Supreme Commander Allied Expeditionary Force of the North African Theatre of Operations.

The scope of Operation *Torch* on 8 November 1942 was, indeed, geographically vast and operationally widespread. There were nine objectives along the 1,000-mile coastal line of north-west Africa that were to be amphibiously seized with the three ports of Casablanca, Oran and Algiers in Morocco and Algeria being the chief targets. After the capture of the three principal Vichy ports, a lengthy, but hasty, overland Allied assault was to commence in mid-November to capture Bizerte and Tunis before General Hans-Jürgen von Arnim's new Panzer army, with 100,000 *Wehrmacht* reinforcements rushed in from Sicily and Italy, could be established in the two port cities serving as a Tunisian bridgehead to maintain a firm Nazi grip on French North Africa. The so-called 'Race for Tunis' was on, which the Allies would lose.

Simultaneous with the Allied Tunisian campaign, Montgomery's Eighth Army would continue its westward movement in an attempt to overtake and destroy Rommel's combined Italian and German forces, retreating from Libya into Tunisia during the third week of January 1943 before they could unite with von Arnim's units. After Second Alamein, even Rommel believed that the continued Axis presence in North Africa was a futile gesture, and he sought to convince Hitler to withdraw the *Panzerarmee Afrika* while there was still a chance. He bluntly informed Hitler that 'if the army remained in North Africa it would be destroyed'. Hitler rejected his field marshal's advice, as von Armin's 5th Panzer Army started its own Tunisian operations at the end of January by seizing the Faïd Pass from a French garrison now in the Allies' camp.

Discussions between the Allied leaders at the Casablanca Conference in January 1943 devised a military strategy for the coming year once the Axis forces were expelled from North Africa. Roosevelt and Churchill wanted to do something further to exploit the impending Allied victory, as an enormous expeditionary force, under Eisenhower, had been amassed there. Churchill, even prior to the conclusion of the

North African campaign, with the capture of Tunis on 9 May 1943, began thinking along the lines of a peripheral strategy in the Mediterranean theatre to reduce Germany's morale and military capability by striking the 'Axis underbelly', considering Sicily a greater prize than Sardinia. Recognising that Hitler and Mussolini's fascist regimes still controlled 6,000 miles of European coastline, US Army planners, after a concurrent build-up of Allied forces in the United Kingdom, wanted a timely invasion of north-west Europe to be undertaken and avoid future detours in the Mediterranean. The British, ever fearful of another continental disaster in north-west Europe, returned to the issue of the vast requirements for Allied shipping and tenuous, lengthy sea lanes.

Although the Allied victory in North Africa had assured control of the Suez Canal, Sicily was still a major enemy-held barrier dividing the Mediterranean Sea from which Axis air and naval power from the island's major airdromes and ports could interdict the sea lanes in those waters. Many of the planners who doubted the wisdom of a Sicilian invasion were won over to a compromise for Operation *Husky*, in that complete Allied control of the Mediterranean Sea would serve as a multiplier for war *matériel* shipping. Safety of the sea lanes through the Straits of Gibraltar would be assured by Sicily's conquest and the more direct maritime route to India and the Pacific through the Suez Canal could be amplified.

Churchill and British planners also postulated that a successful invasion and seizure of Sicily could serve as a later springboard for the invasion of the Italian mainland. Such an event might induce a capitulation of the fascist regime there and a total surrender of the Axis junior partner. British leaders also contended that with Italy's surrender, additional *Wehrmacht* forces would need to be transferred to Southern Europe from both the Russian Front and Southern France, thereby attenuating Nazi strength for the main attack across the English Channel into north-west Europe and the subsequent drive into Germany.

The invasion of Sicily did compete with General Marshall's desire to further concentrate on the build-up of the nascent forces in Britain for a cross-Channel assault. Nonetheless, the US Joint Chiefs of Staff eventually acquiesced to another Mediterranean amphibious operation and favoured Sicily as a target for invasion over either Sardinia or Corsica. Sicily is situated 90 miles off the north coast of Africa, thereby serving as a natural bridge to the European continent. However, in return for the US military leaders undertaking the planned Sicilian invasion, Operation *Husky*, the British at the Casablanca Conference in January 1943 had to whole-heartedly reaffirm the ultimate goal of a cross-Channel invasion for the invasion of north-west Europe in May 1944. On 18 January 1943, the compromise decision between American and British views was to invade Sicily. Operation *Husky* was on. However, it remained unclear as to what to do in the Mediterranean theatre after Sicily, as a fundamental gap still persisted between British and American military strategic views.

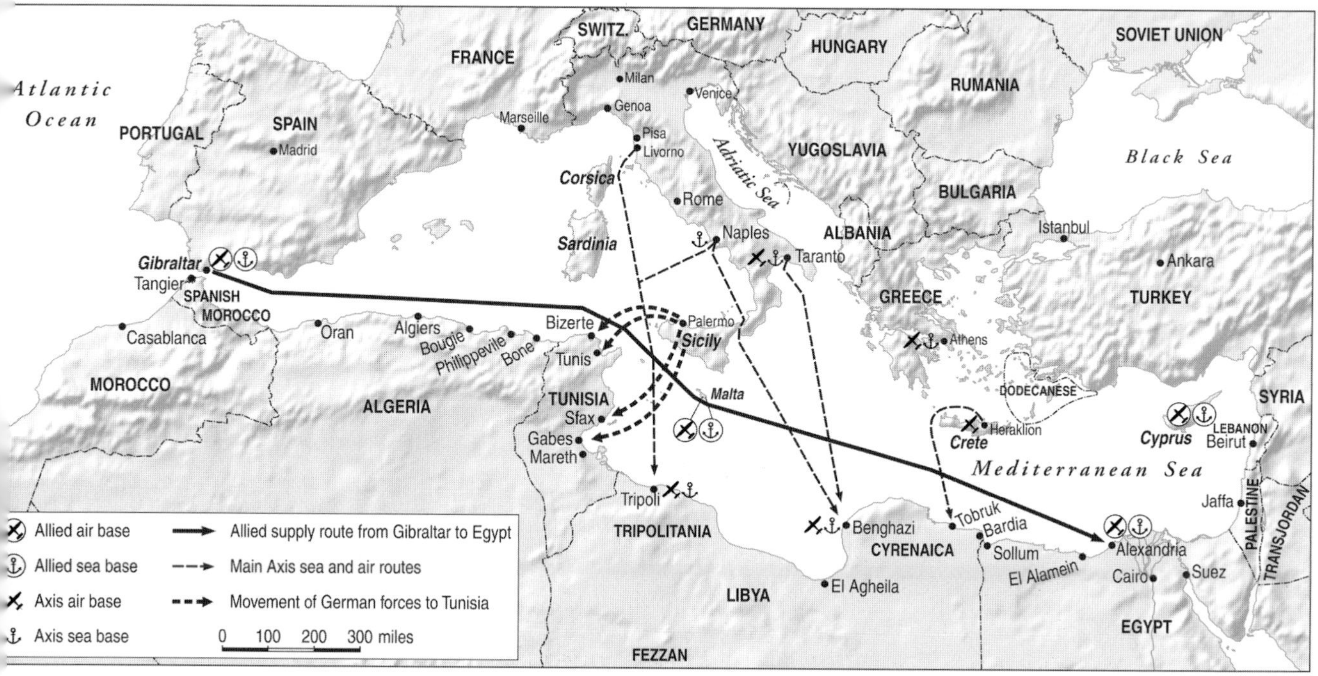


**Mediterranean Theatre of Operations (MTO) 1940–1943.** The island of Sicily and the Strait of Messina had central roles in the MTO from as early as September 1939 until both were captured on 17 August 1943 by the Allies thirty-eight days after the successful amphibious invasion during Operation *Husky* on 10 July 1943. The island's neutralisation and elimination of Italy as an Axis partner were worthy, despite the protests of the US Army command staff and planners, who favoured a more direct, cross-Channel invasion of north-west Europe. Axis lines of communication (LOC), by both air and sea routes, utilised Sicily and the Strait of Messina, to bring supplies and troops to important ports stretching across the entire Mediterranean basin. As shown, these Axis-controlled ports at Tripoli, Benghazi, Tobruk and later Tunis, Bizerte, Gabes and Sfax, would be pivotal for the resupply of the disparate and myriad battlefields of the Middle East and North African littoral, most notably during the Egyptian/Libyan Desert campaign of 1940–1943 and the Tunisian bridgehead reinforcement to resist the Allied movement across French north-west Africa following the first Anglo-American coalition amphibious set of landings during Operation *Torch* on 8 November 1942. Additionally Sicily, with its central Mediterranean location along with numerous Axis airfields and Italian naval bases, had previously interdicted the Allied flow of troops and *matériel* through the Mediterranean Sea, often necessitating the lengthier and more circuitous route around the Cape of Good Hope off South Africa to reach the Middle East and India. The successful Allied destruction of both the Axis 5th Panzer Army, under the command of General Hans-Jürgen von Arnim, and Field Marshal Erwin Rommel's retreating *Panzerarmee Afrika* from El Alamein and across Libya, during the brutal six-month campaign in Tunisia from late November 1942 through to 9 May 1943, enabled the Anglo-American coalition with their new Free French alliance partners to focus military attention onto the 'soft underbelly' of Hitler's Fortress Europe for its next amphibious invasion venture to be launched onto the beaches of south-eastern and eastern Sicily during Operation *Husky*. *(Meridian Mapping)*

American President Franklin D. Roosevelt and British Prime Minister Winston S. Churchill are shown sitting aboard HMS *Prince of Wales* in Placentia Bay, Newfoundland, in August 1941 for joint services. Behind the two political leaders were (*l-to-r*) Admiral Ernest King, USN, Commander-in-Chief, Atlantic Fleet; US Army Chief of Staff General George C. Marshall; and British Chief of the Imperial General Staff (CIGS), General Sir John Dill. Other dignitaries in the background behind King were Harry Hopkins (*left*) and Averill Harriman (*right*). Both of these men were influential advisers and envoys of Roosevelt. They were vital in communicating Britain's willingness to fight to the American president as well as being principal distributors of the $50 billion in Lend-Lease aid to the Allies. At this Atlantic Conference, it was decided to reinforce both England and its ally, the Soviet Union, with American aid, largely through the Lend-Lease, in order to combat the Nazi onslaught. Hopkins also urged Roosevelt to use the US Navy to protect convoys headed to the United Kingdom, even as a non-belligerent. (*NARA*)

Italian fascist dictator Benito Mussolini is shown sitting next to the German Nazi leader Adolf Hitler as both Axis partners rode through a Munich street in 1942. The two formed the Axis 'Pact of Steel', which was signed by Italy's Count Ciano, Joachim von Ribbentrop, and Adolf Hitler on 22 May 1939. However, Italy was a non-belligerent until June 1940, when Mussolini declared war on a near-defeated France. Soon thereafter, the Italian Tenth Army invaded Egypt and spread the European conflict to North Africa and Ethiopia as Churchill chose to combat the weaker Axis partner in those arenas. Eventually, Hitler came to Mussolini's aid in both North Africa and Greece. *(NARA)*

A British Vickers light tank's crewmen are seen scanning the horizon with their binoculars for Italian Tenth Army activity while on reconnaissance in the Western Desert in late 1940. This tank was designed for little else than reconnaissance with its minimal armour (14mm) and armament in the form of only .303 and .5in Vickers machine-guns. It was capable of reaching a top speed of 35mph. As early as 12 June, a day after Italy bombed Malta, British light armoured units began attacking and tracking Italian frontier positions and troop dispositions. The Italians finally crossed the Egyptian frontier in force on 13 September. Mussolini also decided to occupy Greece on 28 October, which was rebuffed by the Greeks. Thus, Mussolini had set into motion a new theatre of operations, the Mediterranean, which Churchill rapidly accepted as to avoid continental combat. *(USAMHI)*

(**Opposite, above**) Italian dead are seen lying beside their destroyed trucks near Derna in January 1941. On 24 January, a British armoured brigade engaged an Italian mechanised column on the Derna-Mechili track, destroying several enemy armoured and 'soft-skinned' vehicles. On 30 January the Italians fled Derna. The way was now open for Lieutenant-General Richard O'Connor to send his Australian infantry west along the coast road towards Benghazi, while his armoured force cut across the desert to trap the retreating Italian Tenth Army and capture it *en masse* at Beda Fomm in early February 1941. *(Library of Congress)*

(**Opposite, below**) General Erwin Rommel, in charge of a new *Wehrmacht* formation, the *Deutsches Afrika Korps* (DAK), is shown standing in his staff car as he accompanied the 15th Panzer Division in its eastward movement rolling up the ground gained by O'Connor's offensive resulting in the investment of Tobruk. Rommel was a decorated First World War veteran and, during the inter-war years, a military author, having written *Infantry Attacks*. After commanding Hitler's bodyguard in Poland, he was awarded with the *Wehrmacht's* 7th Panzer Division, which won much acclaim for its *blitzkrieg*-style dash across northern France in May 1940. Rommel had arrived in Tripoli on 12 February 1941, and the term DAK would become official one week later. Now the desert would provide the ideal terrain for him to exhibit his theories of combined arms in mechanised warfare, where destruction of enemy forces was the aim rather than seizure of locales. *(NARA)*

(**Above**) A dead German soldier is shown lying on the barren, inhospitable Cyrenaican desert terrain with his MP 38 submachine-gun nearby at his feet. The 'butcher's bill' was steep for both sides during the Operation *Crusader* battles. The Germans lost 1,100 killed, 3,400 wounded and 10,100 missing. Their junior Axis partner, Italy, lost 1,200 killed, 2,700 wounded and 19,800 missing. This amounted to a total casualties figure for all Axis forces of 38,300 men, which was equivalent to 32 per cent of the total enemy force committed to the battle. The British had lost 2,900 men killed, 7,300 wounded and 7,500 missing, roughly 15 per cent of the total Eighth Army force engaged. *(Library of Congress)*

A cheerful British soldier, gesturing a 'thumbs-up', is shown escorting a long column of German prisoners to the rear in early winter of 1941. Over 10,000 German and almost 20,000 Italians were captured by Lieutenant-General Alan Cunningham's Eighth Army forces during the two-month-long Operation *Crusader*, which was successful at lifting Rommel's first siege of Tobruk and sent the Axis forces reeling westward to El Agheila. *(USAMHI)*

A sapper from the 2nd South African Infantry Division is shown carrying a stack of landmines to be sown along the outer perimeter of Tobruk in late May 1942. The minefields hastily constructed by the South Africans as well as the defensive entrenchments built during the Gazala Line battles, from 26 May to 17 June, were nothing in comparative strength to what greeted Rommel's first siege the previous year. As a result, the Tobruk garrison was quickly overwhelmed by Axis forces in a matter of days from 17–21 June. This followed the disastrous British retreat back to Egypt from the Gazala Line, which extended from Gazala near the coast west of Tobruk to Bir Hacheim in the south. Rommel had outflanked Lieutenant-General Neil Ritchie's Eighth Army's infantry boxes and armoured formations in a series of fluid engagements at that locale. *(Library of Congress)*

A long column of Allied soldiers, many of them South Africans under the command of Major-General H.B. Klopper, are shown marching into captivity after the port city of Tobruk fell to the Germans with the surrender of the garrison on 21 June 1942. The loss of Tobruk was disastrous with over 33,000 South African, Indians and British troops captured. Also, over 2,000 Allied vehicles were seized and put into Axis service. General Auchinleck, GOC Middle East, had placed the South African Klopper in charge of defending the Tobruk perimeter for a second time. The Tobruk garrison was drawn from a variety of formations and consisted of two brigades from the 2nd South African Infantry Division, the 201st Guards Motor Brigade Group and the 11th Indian Brigade, along with some 'Valentine' and 'Matilda' tank units. Unlike the previous siege, the Tobruk garrison had no aircraft and a dearth of AA artillery, which had bristled throughout the Australian garrison a year earlier. In addition, Klopper, unlike the 9th Australian Division's Morshead before him, had little battle experience and had just recently taken over the 2nd South African Infantry Division after leading a training command. In the early hours of 20 June, Rommel's Panzers made significant breaches across the Allied AT obstacles, which quickly resulted in the Allied collapse of this port that had previously acquired a mythical quality of Allied resistance to Nazi strength. *(USAMHI)*

A sign is shown that marks the railway station at Alamein, which some Australian 'digger' irreverently, but comically, engraved the word 'Heaven' on the masonry wall. On 26 June 1942, Auchinleck cancelled his order for a stand at the Eighth Army desert base of Mersa Matruh after a two-day running battle with the DAK and instructed his formations to retire to the El Alamein line, which had some partial defensive preparations made. *(AWM)*

Prime Minister Winston S. Churchill, seated second from left, during meetings that were conducted in Cairo before his trip to Moscow in August 1942. Seated to the left of Churchill was South African Field Marshal Jan Smuts, a member of Churchill's Imperial War Cabinet. Seated to the right of the prime minister were Miles Lampson, the British Ambassador to Egypt and Sudan, and Richard G. Casey, the British Minister of State for the Middle East. Standing (*left to right*) were Air Chief Marshal Arthur Tedder, General Alan Brooke, Admiral Henry Harwood, General Claude Auchinleck (GOC, Middle East), General Archibald P. Wavell (GOC, India), Charles Wilson (Churchill's personal physician), and Alexander M.G. Cadogan, Permanent Under-Secretary for Foreign Affairs. It was during this trip to Egypt (and then Moscow) that Churchill and Brooke decided to relieve Auchinleck of his Middle East command and replace him with General Harold Alexander. Lieutenant-General Bernard L. Montgomery would take over the command of British Eighth Army. (*NARA*)

Lieutenant-General Bernard L. Montgomery was photographed in the turret of an American-built, British-crewed M3 Medium 'Grant' tank. The arrival of both the 'Lee' and 'Grant' M3 Medium tanks in the desert finally gave the British an armoured vehicle that could duel with the German Panzer IV with some parity, as it had a sponson-mounted 75mm gun and a turret-mounted 37mm gun. The 'Lee' M3 differed from the 'Grant' in that the former had a commander's machine-gun cupola atop the main turret. Prior to being given the desert command, Montgomery was in charge of South-eastern Army in England. Lieutenant-General William 'Strafer' Gott, who had been in the Western Desert since the outbreak of the war and was in command of XIII Corps at Gazala, was supposed to get the Eighth Army command. However, he died when his plane was forced to land and was subsequently machine-gunned by the Germans. Thus, through serendipity, Montgomery took over Eighth Army instead and replaced some of its commanders with men who he knew would re-energise the Dominion troops for the upcoming defensive battle at Alam Halfa (31 August to 4 September 1942) and the offensive at Second Alamein, which was to commence on 23 October. Rommel's plan at the Battle of Alam Halfa was to drive around the southern flank of the British positions along the El Alamein line. The Axis divisions started their approach through the British minefields on the night of 30–31 August. However, the British had intercepted their radio transmissions. Thus, the element of surprise was lost. As the Axis forces retreated after having failed to take the Alam Halfa Ridge and beyond, Montgomery would not commit again to previous folly of massed, rash British armour attacks on Rommel's retiring rearguard, which was often fortified with screens of the tank-busting 88mm AT guns. The second clash on the El Alamein battlefield, at Alam Halfa, ended by the evening of 5 September, by which time Rommel extricated all of his forces. The German Field Marshal's troops captured the Himeimat Ridge in the south as his sole gain. Montgomery was not displeased with the Axis possession of this terrain feature, since it was from this location that the enemy would overlook British military deception ploys with 'dummy' preparations that would enable the enemy to conclude that the main Allied counter-offensive, when launched, would be hurled from the south. *(NARA)*.

At 2115 hours on the night of 23 October 1942, Montgomery's Eighth Army fired the largest artillery barrage seen during the Second World War up until that time to herald the commencement of Operation *Lightfoot*. Here, Royal Artillery Ordnance, QF, 4.5in anti-aircraft (AA) guns fired during the night as part of the bombardment. On average, the Royal Artillery's 4.5in AA guns fired 102 rounds per gun per day over the initial twelve days of fighting during Second Alamein. Over one million rounds were fired by the British guns, which included the 25-pounders and 5.5in weapons as well. The artillery-fire was highly concentrated and targeted for the Allied shells to simultaneously land on the *Panzerarmee Afrika*'s positions across the 40-mile front. The Desert Air Force sent in its Boston and Wellington bombers to intensify the Allied bombardment at 2200 hours. After a five-minute lull in Eighth Army's artillery barrage, new timed concentrations from Allied field-guns opened up, but this time eight brigades of XXX Corps infantry leaped from their slit trenches to begin Operation *Lightfoot*. The Second Battle of El Alamein had started. The Axis defenders were concussed, stunned and deafened by the intense bombardment. Much of the *Panzerarmee*'s vital communication links were destroyed. *(Library of Congress)*

(**Opposite, above**) A Royal Artillery BL 4.5in medium field cannon (not to be confused with the QF, 4.5in anti-aircraft gun) crew of the 64th Regiment is shown preparing for a daylight fire mission on Axis targets that were being relayed via a telephone line to the gunner in the foreground. This field cannon was designed as a replacement for the older 60-pounder and was deployed against Rommel's Axis forces in the El Alamein battles from June to November 1942. *(NARA)*

(**Opposite, below**) A British 6-pounder AT gun is shown being situated for action against Axis armour. This excellent AT gun arrived in North Africa in mid-1942 in time for the Gazala battle and proved vital at both Alamein battles and Alam Halfa against German and Italian tanks. The 6-pounder shell could penetrate 50mm of armour at approximately 1,650yds. American factories made a 57mm AT gun, which had the same design as the British 6-pounder. The arrival of the British 6-pounder also enabled the 25-pounder field artillery piece to revert to its primary function rather than in an AT role due to the obsolete performance of the 2-pounder AT gun. *(NARA)*

181810.

(**Opposite, above**) A British truck is shown towing a 40mm Bofors gun past a dead German soldier as the Eighth Army advanced westward against the retreating Axis forces after the Second Battle of El Alamein. This fine weapon was originally designed for the Swedish Navy in the mid-1930s and was subsequently manufactured under licensing agreements by several combatant and non-combatant nations. The gun was ideally suited for its anti-aircraft (AA) role in that it had a high rate of fire at 120 rounds per minute. As shown, there was a single-barrel gun on a mobile mounting for land use, while for naval use, a dual configuration barrel was manufactured. Approximately 2,000lb in weight, this AA gun, although vehicle-towed, was highly mobile. *(NARA)*

(**Opposite, below**) Allied infantrymen of the British Eighth Army are seen climbing aboard a disabled Italian M13/40 tank during the fighting around El Alamein from July to November 1942. The M13/40 was one of the least effective tanks during the desert conflict, although it was available to the Italians in relatively large numbers. It was slow in cross-country speed. Although it possessed an accurate 47mm main turret gun that fired armour-piercing rounds, it was unable to compete with the faster and more heavily armoured tanks of the British Eighth Army at this time. *(NARA)*

(**Above**) Allied infantrymen of the British Eighth Army were photographed taking cover at the side of an abandoned German Mk III Panzer during Operation *Supercharge* on 2 November 1942. Montgomery also heralded this attack by another British artillery salvo of 360 guns and a Desert Air Force bombardment. *Supercharge*'s intent was to penetrate Rommel's main line south of the salient previously formed by the 9th Australian Division. Montgomery used his Australian contingents, beginning on the night of 24 October, to begin 'crumbling' Axis defences on the northern or right flank of the offensive towards the sea with the intent of seizing the coastal road by surprising the enemy. The Aussies succeeded in capturing many strategic battlefield targets. By late morning on 2 November, some elements of the British 1st Armoured Division had made a limited breakthrough into the desert following up on the excellent night-fighting efforts of the 51st Highland and British 50th Infantry Divisions, a Maori unit from the New Zealand Division, and the heroic sacrifice of the 9th Armoured Brigade to clear the minefields defended by remaining units of the German 15th Panzer and Italian Littorio Divisions. However, the Allies had not achieved a complete breakthrough in the Axis lines during *Supercharge*. Eighth Army did, indeed, form a new salient though, which would compel Rommel to counter-attack. *(NARA)*

General Ritter von Thoma (*right*) is shown in his combat uniform at an informal meeting with General Bernard Montgomery (*wearing pullover on left*) at Eighth Army desert headquarters after the former's capture by the 11th Hussars in one of the final tank actions of the Second Battle of El Alamein on 4 November 1942. Prior to North Africa, von Thoma was considered a specialist in mechanised force tactics, having commanded both the 6th and 20th Panzer Divisions in Russia. Interestingly, in October 1940, von Thoma was sent to North Africa to assess whether the *Wehrmacht* should assist the Italians in driving the British out of Egypt. He advocated sending four Panzer divisions to North Africa, which was twice the number eventually dispatched to Tripoli in order to aid the faltering Italians after their rout at Beda Fomm in early February 1941. Von Thoma took over the DAK, under Rommel's overall *Panzerarmee Afrika* command, after General Walther Nehring was wounded at Alam Halfa in August 1942. When Rommel was evacuated to Germany in late September 1942 to restore his health, General Stumme arrived from Russia to take over for Rommel, but he died of a heart attack at the onset of Second Alamein after his staff car drove into an Australian patrol. The *Panzerarmee Afrika* was briefly leaderless, when von Thoma took it over pending Rommel's return to the battlefield. The DAK command then reverted back to von Thoma. (*NARA*)

In late January 1942, Brigadier-General Dwight D. Eisenhower (*left*), the new Chief of War Plans for the Army's General Staff, was appointed by the Army Chief of Staff, General George C. Marshall (*right*). This partnership forged an American blueprint for US Army operations in the European Theatre of Operations (ETO). Eisenhower wrote at that time, 'We've got to go to Europe and fight ... We've got to quit wasting resources all over the world ... and still worse ... wasting time ...' Marshall could not have agreed more with his protégé's concepts as both argued for an early infusion of American soldiers to staging areas in Britain in 1942 (Operation *Bolero*) as part of a plan for a cross-Channel invasion of France in April 1943 (Operation *Roundup*). The British partner in the alliance demurred at another European invasion after Dunkirk, Narvik and Greece, as well as what was to become another disaster, Dieppe, in August 1942. The British Chief, Imperial General Staff (CIGS) General Alan Brooke harboured grave reservations that if British troops invaded continental Europe prematurely, they would be hastily expelled yet again with unacceptably high casualties. (*NARA*)

(**Above**) Two corporals from the 1st Ranger Battalion are shown covering a French gun battery above Arzew Harbour to the east of Oran on D-Day. The ranger in the foreground was armed with the relatively new M1 semi-automatic Garand rifle, while the one behind him was aiming his Springfield M1903 bolt-action rifle, which although very accurate, firing a heavy calibre round could not match the M1 Garand in rate of fire. *(NARA)*

(**Opposite, above**) A Vichy French White-Laffy armoured car of the *Chasseurs d-Afrique* is shown sitting disabled after coming under fire from an American 37mm anti-tank gun of the 26th Regimental Combat Team (RCT) on D-Day at El Ancor, inland from Les Andalouses landing beach, west of Oran. The Djebel Murdajajdao, which was situated east-to-west from Les Andalouses to the western outskirts of Oran, is shown in the background. *(NARA)*

(**Opposite, below**) After the Central Task Force disembarked soldiers of the US 1st Infantry Division to seize Oran from beaches east and west of the port city, large numbers of Vichy French troops surrendered. Here they are shown being guarded by two American sergeants in the foreground and a few more GIs in the background. *(NARA)*

American soldiers are photographed climbing down both cargo nets (*background*) and a ladder suspended from a hull hatch door of a troop transport of the Eastern Task Force (*foreground*) into waiting British-crewed landing craft for the run-in towards landing beaches around Algiers, 270 miles east of Oran. The city of Algiers was spread out over a 16-mile-long bay and had a civilian population of 300,000, and the landing beaches were well to the east and west of the port. After reaching shore, the Allied landing forces were instructed to move inland quickly to seize the airfields at Blida and Maison Blanche, respectively. *(USAMHI)*

(**Opposite, above**) American troops are shown disembarking from British-crewed landing craft later in the day on D-Day as a transport and another approaching landing craft were in the background. The 168th Infantry Regiment of the US 34th Division was to land at *White* and *Green* beaches in the *Beer* sector but was scattered in the darkness early on D-Day along 15 miles of Algerian coastline. The US 39th Infantry Regiment of the 9th Division was to land at the most eastern point of the amphibious assault, at Surcouf. *(USAMHI)*

(**Opposite, below**) An American M3 37mm AT gun-crew is shown watching for attacking Axis armour from a minimally-concealed position on typical Tunisian rock-strewn desert mixed with scrub as the battle at Sidi bou Zid was about to erupt on 14 February 1943. During von Arnim's counter-offensive, the Americans around Sidi bou Zid lost over fifty-five half-tracks, twenty-five artillery pieces and twenty trucks due to poor deployment and lack of suitable cover. The 37mm AT gun was woefully inadequate against German armour at this stage of the war. *(NARA)*

149055

(**Above**) A reconnaissance Jeep with its three crew members that survived the fighting at Sidi bou Zid in mid-February is shown above. The vehicle and crew were surrounded on Djebel Lessouda by von Arnim's Panzer forces for three days before making their escape on 17 February 1943. *(USAMHI)*

(**Opposite, above**) In order to defend against the sorties flown by the *Luftwaffe* in support of the 10th Panzer Division's battlegroup thrust at El Guettar on 23 March 1943, a 40mm Bofors M1 anti-aircraft (AA) gun was deployed there. The crew attempted to have somewhat of a dug-in position on the hard, rock-laden Tunisian desert floor with sandbags placed on the lip of the entrenchment. *(USAMHI)*

(**Opposite, below**) American combat engineers, using visual inspection and prodding of the ground with a long bayonet where buried mines were suspected, try to clear the railway station at Kasserine in late February 1943 as part of II Corps counter-offensive after the stinging Axis defeats just several days before. *(USAMHI)*

KASSERINE

171896

(**Opposite, above**) Two officers (*foreground*) of the US 601st Tank Destroyer Battalion are shown poring over a map in front of their M3 command half-track at El Guettar in late March 1943. Two Jeeps and a M3 75mm GMC tank destroyer are seen to the rear of this reconnaissance half-track. At El Guettar, the M3 75mm GMC tank played a pivotal role in halting the advance of a 10th Panzer Division battlegroup. *(NARA)*

(**Opposite, below**) In early May 1943, a patrol from the British East Surrey Regiment is shown moving in front of a Churchill heavy infantry tank through the typical Tunisian countryside near the base of Longstop Hill, which was the scene of previous heavy combat in December 1942. *(Author's Collection)*

(**Above**) A patrol from the US 60th Infantry regiment of the 9th Division was photographed coursing through the hillsides 10 miles outside of Bizerte on 7 May 1943, the day before the Axis bridgehead port fell to the Americans. *(USAMHI)*

MAISON SADOK BENDIABER
FOURNISSEUR de LARMEE
LIMONADE
Bière
T42768

(**Opposite, above**) Infantrymen of the US 9th Division are seen walking down tree-lined streets of Bizerte with their bayonets fixed as they received sporadic sniper fire. After fighting in the northern Tunisian hills, this type of urban fighting was unusual and would prompt mock urban combat training for reinforcements as they arrived in North Africa. *(USAMHI)*

(**Above**) Australian gunners, who were now long-term veterans in Montgomery's Eighth Army, are shown posing in front of their 25-pounder field artillery piece as they approached the Mareth Line in southern Tunisia. *(USAMHI)*

(**Opposite, below**) A British Universal or Bren carrier is shown entering the town of Mareth, situated between Medenine to the south and Gabes to the north, in southern Tunisia. The term 'Universal', applied to the carrier, was apt since it could be used for a variety of combat functions from simply moving infantry or being armed with a Bren light machine-gun, a Boys anti-tank rifle, and a mortar. *(NARA)*

A sketch of the Italian fascist dictator, Benito Mussolini, is shown lying trampled along a roadside with spent shell casings accompanying it as Axis forces continued their retreat towards Bizerte in the spring of 1943. The Axis defeat was an incredible blow to Italy and rocked the prestige of the pretentious Mussolini. The Italians had lost their African colonies along with any imperial delusions that they harboured before the war in North Africa, Abyssinia and Italian Somaliland began in earnest in December 1940. As Allied bombing of Italy intensified from newly-constructed North African airfields, Mussolini and his fascist party seemed increasingly impotent in the eyes of ordinary Italians, who would soon begin their war-stricken ordeal on their own soil. *(USAMHI)*

British and American leaders who had forged a victory with Operation *Torch* and the victory in Tunisia after the six-month campaign are shown conferring in North Africa in May 1943 for the final planning of the next Allied endeavour, Operation *Husky*, the invasion of Sicily. British Prime Minister Winston Churchill was seated at the table with his trademark cigar (*centre*). The trio behind him (*from left to right*) included: Air Chief Marshal Arthur Tedder of the Royal Air Force (RAF); Admiral Andrew Cunningham, Commander of the Mediterranean Fleet; General Harold Alexander, Commander-in-Chief (C-in-C) 18th Army Group. To the far left of Churchill was Anthony Eden, Britain's Minister for War, and General Alan Brooke (awarded field marshal rank in January 1944), Commander Imperial General Staff (CIGS). Seated to the right of Churchill were Generals George C. Marshall, US Army Chief of Staff, and Dwight D. Eisenhower, Supreme Commander of Allied Forces. Standing to the far right was General Bernard L. Montgomery, C-in-C British Eighth Army. Not shown were the US Navy's Vice Admiral H. Kent Hewitt, the senior naval commander of the Western Naval Task Force, and Rear Admirals Alan G. Kirk, Richard L. Conolly and John L. Hall, the commanders of landing Task Forces 85, 86 and 81, respectively. (*Author's Collection*)

(**Above**) During the early days of July 1943, infantrymen of the US 3rd Division are shown boarding barges that will take them to transports offshore from Bizerte Harbour that will become part of the invasion armada for Operation *Husky*, the invasion of Sicily. General Lucian Truscott took over command of these combat veterans of Operation *Torch* and the Tunisian campaign. He led them superbly during the amphibious assault at Licata, the farthest west of the US Army's sector during the invasion of Sicily and throughout the thirty-eight-day campaign, culminating in the seizure of Messina. *(USAMHI)*

(**Opposite, above**) British infantrymen of the 2nd Seaforth Highlanders are shown boarding Landing Craft, Infantry (LCI) transports at Sousse, a Tunisian port, on 5 July 1943, for transit to their landing beaches on Eastern Sicily five days later. The assault beaches for Montgomery's Eighth Army spanned from Pachino and Cape Passero in the south to the outskirts of Syracuse to the north. *(NARA)*

(**Opposite, below**) A Royal Navy transport is seen as part of the convoy armada steamed in line with a wide array of naval vessels for Operation *Husky*. Transports, in addition to having left Tunisian ports, sailed from Egypt, the United Kingdom and the eastern United States, comprising the vast invasion armada headed for the eastern and southern coastal areas of Sicily. *(NARA)*

249
299
132

# Chapter Two

# Terrain, Fortifications and Installations

A military theatre's terrain dictates tactics. Terrain features impact enormously on the development of defensive fortifications as well contributing greatly to the decisions regarding offensive thrusts. Military geography affects strategic decision-making and logistical planning as it examines how locales are interrelated to one another in regards to distance, size, value of the site, and the suitability of lines of communication (LOC). The thirty-eight-day campaign for Sicily, from 10 July to 17 August 1943, would be continually impacted by both the island's terrain and geography.

Sicily, being almost 10,000 square miles in size, is the largest island in the central Mediterranean Sea, comparable in size to Vermont, Wales or Switzerland. Within its roughly isosceles triangular shape, Sicily's terrain is mostly hilly and mountainous and the island's volcanic activity is intense. The Plain of Catania in the east is the only wide valley region, while some additional narrow coastal plains on the eastern and southern shores are extant. The northern and southern coasts are each about 170 miles long while the eastern coast is 110 miles in length.

Over the centuries, the island had been mostly deforested and replaced with cultivated fields, wherever possible. The climate of Sicily is typically Mediterranean with mild and wet winters while the summers are hot and arid. During the months of July and August, temperatures can exceed 110° Fahrenheit. There are a number of neighbouring islands, including Pantelleria and Lampedusa to the south, the former of which is also volcanic. Both islands became fortified with the outbreak of the Second World War.

Sicily is just 2 miles across the northern part of the Strait of Messina from Reggio di Calabria on the Italian mainland. Messina was obviously the Allies' most strategic target to seize as it was the Axis logistical connection, via a ferry service, to the Italian mainland. A rapid Allied occupation of Messina could conceivably trap the Axis combatants on Sicily from effective escape or relief. The island is also just about 90 miles away from Cape Bon on the tip of Tunisia. Along with its central location within the Mediterranean Sea, these geographical facts enabled Sicily to play an

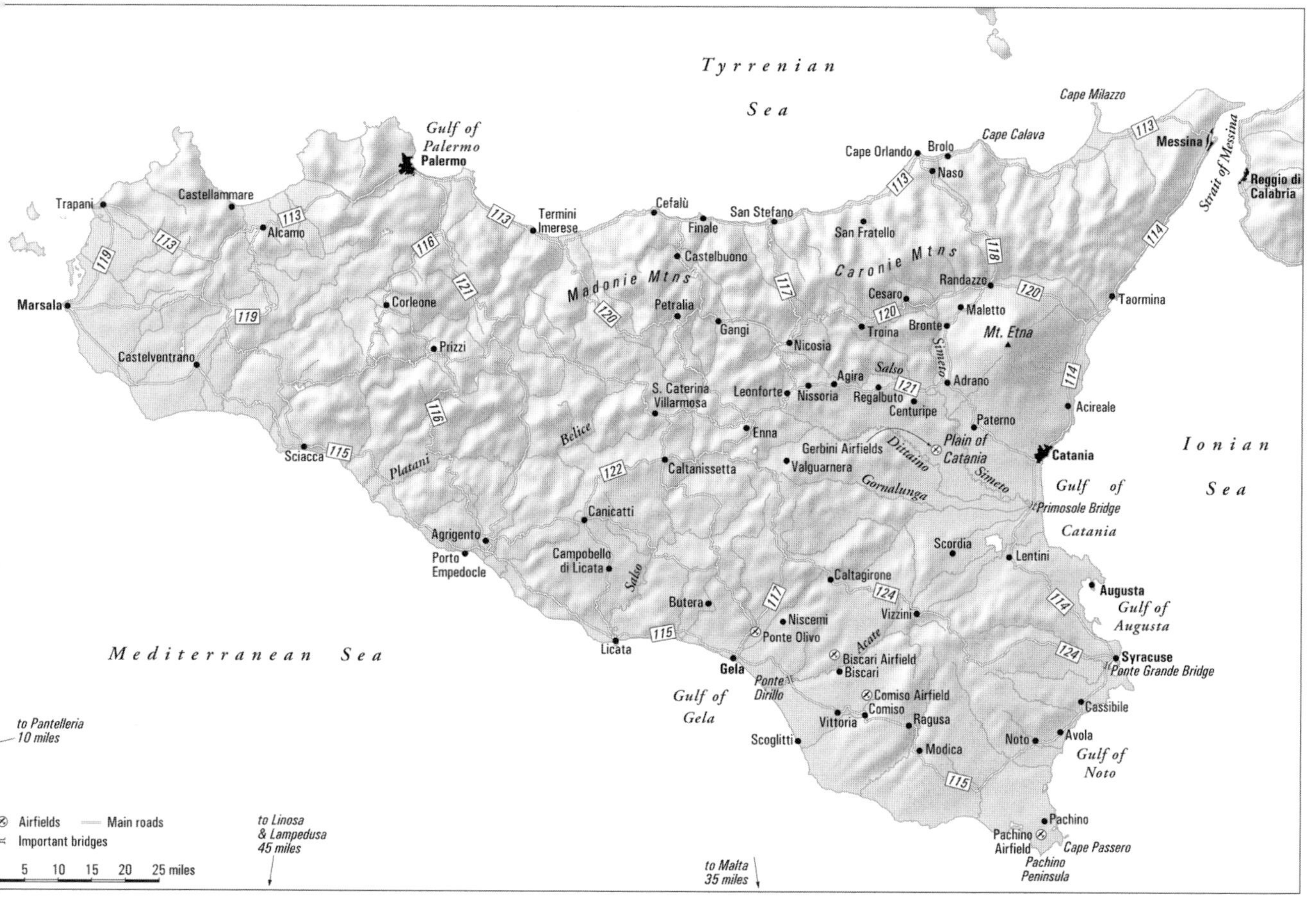


**Sicilian locales.** The important locales on the island of Sicily are depicted on the above map and also demonstrate pivotal terrain features, highways, railways and Axis airfields. The beaches of south-eastern and eastern Sicily, in the Gulf of Gela, along the Pachino Peninsula, and the Gulf of Noto, respectively are shown. The Mount Etna massif is shown, which played such an extremely major role in determining the strategic moves of Montgomery's British Eighth Army and the Axis defence lines of Catania and Messina. Also, the Caronie and Madonie mountain ranges across northern Sicily would provide rugged terrain for elements of Patton's Seventh Army to move across and would strategically become an Axis 'force multiplier', since the mechanised nature of the American force would be limited in its drive from Palermo to Messina. Also, the airfields at Ponte Olivo, Biscari, Comiso, Pachino and the Gerbini complex on the Plain of Catania would be vital objectives for early Allied seizure to provide air bases for North African Allied Air Force tactical fighter-bomber squadrons to support the advancing infantry and interdict Axis reinforcement of the island. The paucity of major highways on Sicily would determine the major routes of advance for the elements of the two Allied armies as the US Provisional Corps would initially move on coastal Highway 115 to the west to first Porto Empedocle and Sciacca and then through western Sicily's mountainous terrain on Highways 116 and 119 to the capital port-city of Palermo on the island's northern coast. The 3rd Division, after Palermo's capture, would relieve the northern coastal moves of the US 1st and 45th Divisions, and make a contentious advance along Highway 113 against a tenacious and withdrawing Axis foe that used demolitions to perfection. The ceding of Highway 124 from the US 45th Division to British 30th Corps' formations, would compel the Americans to return to the Gela beachhead in order to then move to the left of the US 1st Division for the advance north. The east-west running Highways 120 and 121 would become the arteries for the US 1st Infantry and the 1st Canadian Divisions to move eastwards from Petralia and Leonforte, respectively, onto Randazzo and Adrano, both major road networks connecting these latter locales to the strategic prize of Messina and neutralisation of the Strait of Messina. After the Allied rendezvous at Randazzo, the British 13th Corps would continue its advance north from Catania through Acireale and Taormina to Messina. *(Meridian Mapping)*

important role in the early years of the Second World War by allowing the Axis partners to interdict Allied shipping through the Mediterranean Sea to the Middle East, and especially to the besieged island of Malta, lying directly due south of Licata and Gela on Sicily's southern coast.

The rise of fascism in Europe in the twentieth century soon evolved into another occupation of Sicily. However, this time by Mussolini's Italian Army. Mussolini's fascist government had transformed Sicily into a gigantic, stationary aircraft carrier for fleets of *Luftwaffe* and Italian aircraft to fly sorties from. With the Italian dictator entering as a belligerent into the Second World War in early June 1940, Mussolini subjected the inhabitants of Sicily first to both an unwelcome presence of *Wehrmacht* and *Luftwaffe* units and the curse of another possible invasion, this time by the Allies, that would assail their shores in the future. In addition, the Italian Navy had major bases at the ports of Augusta-Syracuse, Palermo and Messina.

With its central Mediterranean location and proximity to the European and African continents, war and conquest had been ubiquitous for the Sicilians over the centuries. The result of the repetitive conquests and occupations was a *mélange* of ethnicities and cultures from which Sicilian cities still possessed architectural edifices from past Hellenic and Roman glory. The initial Hellenic colonisation was near Messina in roughly 760 BC, which spawned the Greek independent city-state of Syracuse well to the south along Sicily's east coast at the base of the Gulf of Augusta. Roman domination and Sicilian enslavement to an Italian central government occurred as an outgrowth of the Second Punic War over five centuries later. Other waves of conquest including Moslem, Norman, and other European dynasties successively occurred until the mid-nineteenth century when General Giuseppe Garibaldi defeated his Italian mainland foe from Naples at Calatatimi to the south-west of Palermo, the capital of the island, on 15 May 1860. With repeated episodes of Sicily's invasion and consequent subjugation, the dominant defence modality among the island's inhabitants was to situate their collective dwellings, varying in size from villages to cities, perched high along mountain tops and ridgelines to serve as a topographic fortifier from the invader.

The first phase of the plan to capture Sicily called for preparatory bombardment measures by Allied air and naval forces to gain air superiority and to neutralise the Axis naval presence in the Mediterranean. Many of the German and Italian airbases and port facilities on Pantelleria and Sicily had been bombed prior to the amphibious invasion, necessitating the planes and warships being withdrawn to safer bases in Italy and southern France. Pantelleria lay to the south-west of Sicily and to Malta's north-west. The heavy Allied air and naval bombardment on Pantelleria, Operation *Cork-screw*, began on 18 May 1943. The bombing continued with 3,500 planes dropping almost 5,000 tons of bombs on Pantelleria. By early June, the port was in ruins and the town destroyed. Italian casualties were few but damage to housing, roads and communications was extensive. Other islands in the Pelagian archipelago, Lampedusa and Linosa located in the Mediterranean Sea between Malta to the east and Tunisia to the west, were similarly bombarded in early June.

Pantelleria was assaulted and captured by elements of the British 1st Division on 11 June 1943. The Allied ships dropped anchor 8 miles from the island's harbour entrance and landing craft were lowered. Pantelleria was hardly seen as it was obscured by a cloud of haze and dust caused by the intense Allied bombardment. The garrison on Pantelleria surrendered within hours of the amphibious landing. Lampedusa and Linosa also fell with little resistance.

The airdromes on Pantelleria and Lampedusa now became Allied Air Forces' tactical support bases. On 20 June, British aircraft began to operate from Lampedusa and six days later a group of US P-40 Warhawk fighters was based at Pantelleria. The Axis airfields on Sicily, Sardinia and southern Italy continued to be targets to interdict Axis air assets with the upcoming amphibious assault planned for 10 July 1943. A successful invasion of Sicily, Operation *Husky*, would first require a substantial reduction of the Axis air strength based on the island.

Sicily housed nineteen airdromes plus ten additional landing strips, none of which were more than 15 miles from the shore. The north-western edge of the Plain of Catania had five airfields in the Gerbini complex that the Allied Air Forces would eventually have to occupy to provide tactical fighter and fighter-bomber air support for operations in north-eastern Sicily to seize Messina. Without Allied control of the Plain of Catania, a northward advance to Messina would be thwarted by the Axis defence, largely due to a lack of tactical air support fields. Hence the need for Montgomery's British Eighth Army to land on Sicily's eastern coast to advance on the Plain of Catania. Sicily's other major Axis airfields, in addition to the Gerbini complex, included the ones in the Gela sector at Biscari, Comiso and Ponte Olivo in the eastern half of the island, which Air Chief Marshal (ACM) Arthur Tedder was eager to quickly seize to base his tactical air assets to cover the assault beaches and the drive inland. This would necessitate additional Allied amphibious assaults by Patton's US Seventh Army along the beaches of the Gulf of Gela.

Two topographic areas stood out in the Allied planning to quickly move from the assault beaches along the southern and eastern narrow coastal strips northwards to Messina. The first, because of its airfields, was the Plain of Catania, which was a broad 18 mile by 12 mile area comprising marshy, malaria-infested lowland situated to Mount Etna's south. This valley region received copious mountain runoff, notably in the form of the Simeto River, which drained into the Gulf of Catania. The second was the Caronie Mountains, ranging in height from 4,500 to 5,500 feet, in the north-east are the highest and are topped by Mount Etna. This active and large volcano was vast in size, standing on a base of 20 miles in diameter and rising to over 10,000 feet in height.

An invading army that wanted to drive north from Syracuse to Messina had to either force through a narrow corridor between the eastern face of Mount Etna and the sea utilising the only highway, Route 114, or to move west of the Plain of Catania to as far inland as Leonforte and then trek across the Simeto River valley to the east-west Route 120, thereby attacking around the prominence from the west. This is what confronted Montgomery and his Eighth Army in both planning and execution phases of the invasion of Sicily.

The mountainous terrain of Sicily would be a 'force multiplier' for the Axis since it would enable the defenders to concentrate their troops on a narrow front. Also, the highly defensible hill towns and mountain villages could serve as perfect artillery observation points viewing the surrounding lowlands for any Allied movement. The entire northern coast of Sicily consists of steep and precipitous cliffs facing the sea. The rugged terrain would hamper the manoeuvreability of Allied mechanised armoured units and towed artillery, both of which had played decisive roles in the victories in Egypt, Libya and French north-west Africa. Additionally, Sicily's shortage of good inland roads would add to this tactical dilemma.

The heavy fortifications at Messina ruled out a direct blow there and similar defences ringed the naval facilities of Syracuse, Catania, Augusta and Palermo. These comprised effectively organised anti-shipping and anti-aircraft artillery facing a potential Allied seaward thrust on the defence locales. British Admiral Cunningham, well aware of the Royal Navy's disastrous Dardanelles forced passage against well-armed Turkish forts in 1915, did not want to repeat such a misadventure. These facts compelled Montgomery to land his Eighth Army assault forces at relatively undefended beaches on the south-eastern coast of Sicily in the Gulf of Noto extending from Cape Passero in the south to Cape Muuro di Porco, just to the south of Syracuse. With an unreliable coastal militia manning these Italian naval base defensive positions and a lack of defences against a landward attack, Montgomery planned to seize Syracuse with a coastal march of his infantry, preceded the night before by an air-landing glider assault (Operation *Ladbroke*) against the nearby Ponte Grande Bridge. Patton's Seventh Army would land along Sicily's southern coastal beaches in the Gulf of Gela from Licata in the west to Scoglitti in the east. Allied troops would land against little opposition except that from fixed coastal defences manned by poorly trained and motivated Italian troops. Many fortifications along the coastal areas lacked sufficient garrisons, weapons or troop shelters. At all assault sites, the Allies would have to deal with landmines and concealed positions in addition to the concrete pillboxes. Additionally, at Gela, where the veteran US 1st Infantry Division landed, mines and sandbars slowed the landing of armour and artillery, enabling the unleashing of Axis counter-attacks on the ground on 10 and 11 July and in the skies above the invasion armada.

From a hydrographic standpoint, Sicily's shoreline had numerous narrow coastal areas, variable in length ranging from hundreds of yards to many miles that were composed of soft beach sand and shingle along the island's eastern and southern shores. The Allies would have to come ashore along the mostly unfortified stretches of coastline, as the Axis had constructed numerous defensive works proximate to the water's edge. Because amphibious techniques and beach maintenance with the unloading supplies were still rudimentary, the Allies wanted to capture at least one port at once. As it turned out, Syracuse provided that strategic aim, following a 1st British Airborne assault on the Ponte Grande Bridge on the outskirts of the port with subsequent relief by advancing elements of the British 5th Infantry Division. Due to the above-mentioned terrain features, an Allied advance to Messina was planned for movement along the island's eastern coast from amphibious landings along the Gulf of Noto in the south-east through terrain bordering the more northerly Gulfs of Augusta and Catania and, then, northward, paralleling the eastern face of Mount Etna, onto Messina.

Along the coastal area, the highways were adequate for motor transport, but in the interior they were poorly surfaced, creating extensive dust clouds on the narrow roads with sharp curves and steep grades that would contribute to vehicular traffic congestion. The roads servicing the numerous villages, towns and small cities were all usually situated atop hills or mountains for defence. These roadways were more suitably designed for walking and/or mule or donkey carts. After the initial Allied landings, the deployment of both combatants' forces was severely delayed because of narrow, winding roads, which especially hampered the heavy German Mk VI 'Tiger' tanks to manoeuvre effectively.

Immediately after the three US divisions landed at separate sites along the southern shoreline in the Gulf of Gela, the terrain on the Plain of Gela proved to be suitable for a Panzer counter-attack against the US 1st Division's slowly-developing beachhead. However, since the Plain of Gela was in close proximity to offshore Allied warships, heavy and accurate naval gunfire caused severe losses among the German Panzers deployed out in the open and halted the counter-attack.

Sicily's topographical features, along with the Axis fortifications, minefields, and poor road infrastructure interiorly on the island, would accentuate the maxim that the nature of a theatre's terrain lies at the heart of military tactics. The Allies, after the successful amphibious landings, would have to both adapt their tactics as well as implement major changes in their military plan and deployment of forces in order to reach and seize the strategic prize of Messina, thus achieving yet another conquest of Sicily.

Fortunately, for the Allied amphibious assault troops, the conduct of the Italian garrison troops exhibited extreme demoralisation. There were mass desertions from posts often with Italian troops searching for Allied units to surrender to. By the end of the first week of the invasion, the US Seventh Army had herded over 20,000 prisoners-of-war into temporary stockades with at least 25 per cent being conscripted Sicilians who were forced to serve as an arm of the local militia to combat the landings.

An aerial view of the island of Pantelleria, to Sicily's south-west, under high-altitude Allied Air Forces' bombardment during Operation *Corkscrew*, which commenced on 18 May 1943. The North African Strategic Air Force (NASAF), under Lieutenant-General Carl Spaatz, comprised B-17 heavy bombers, medium bombers and fighter escorts, pounded the island for over three weeks. Mussolini had begun fortifying Pantelleria in the latter part of the 1930s to balance the British presence on the nearby island of Malta, south of Sicily. After hostilities commenced, Pantelleria became a major base for German and Italian aircraft. It had a garrison of about 10,000 men under Italian Admiral Gino Pavesi. General Eisenhower wanted this island, along with the nearby Pelagian islands of Lampedusa and Linosa located in the Mediterranean Sea between Malta to the east and Tunisia to the west, captured before any amphibious landings on Sicily. It was anticipated by the Allied High Command that the massive air assault would demoralise the Italian garrison and make an amphibious assault by the British 1st Infantry Division more effective. Lampedusa and Linosa surrendered on 12 June without any significant fighting. *(NARA)*

The Sicilian airfield at Trapani/Milo, located to the west of Palermo on the island's north-western tip, during an attack by high-altitude Allied B-17 and B-24 heavy bombers from North Africa during the day and RAF Wellington squadrons operating at night from bases on Malta. Over seventy Axis planes were caught on the ground during this daytime raid with thirty being destroyed. In addition, the main runway traversing the airfield from the upper left to the middle of the photograph was also heavily cratered. Total Axis aircraft destroyed or damaged on the ground on Sicily during the Allied bombing campaign numbered well over 200 planes destroyed. The air attacks on the Axis's Sicilian airfields by B-17 heavy bomber groups commenced in May 1943 as the Allied leaders were concerned about major losses among the ships of the invasion armada if these air bases were not neutralised. The Gerbini airfield complex, the largest on Sicily with major and satellite airstrips, was evacuated by the *Luftwaffe* by the second week of July 1943, as it could not be repaired from damage by the time of the Operation *Husky* amphibious assaults. *(NARA)*

(**Above**) A B-17 heavy bomber is shown flying over Messina, recognised easily from the air with its 'fish-hook' port facility topographic feature, after the invasion commenced. The Allied Air Forces' bombing of Messina bore a certain resemblance to raids conducted against German cities. Axis observers noted that the harbour was in flames along with about half of the city destroyed, producing a sense of terror in the port's inhabitants causing a panicked exodus to the ferries to get to the Italian mainland. Although there was heavy AA fire against the Allied aircraft, few bombers were brought down due to ineffective aim and fire control of the weapons. Palermo, the Sicilian capital, was also targeted for heavy bomber raids beginning soon after the invasion. Palermo was among the four communication centres of Sicily, which included Catania, Randazzo and Messina. Likewise, the raids on Palermo produced chaos and isolation in the capital on the northern coast. *(NARA)*

(**Opposite, above**) Smoke and dust emanate from the smouldering ruins of Pantelleria's port facilities following four days of intensified bombardment from 7–11 June 1943. On 11 June 1943, twenty-four days after Operation *Corkscrew* commenced, the British 1st Infantry Division landed and the Italian garrison quickly surrendered. *(NARA)*

(**Opposite, below**) A Nazi aeroplane, probably a dual-engine Ju-88 medium bomber, based on Sicily is shown exploding in flames during a low-level Allied fighter bomber sweep of an Axis airfield. The Ju-88 was developed by the *Luftwaffe* as a high-speed level and dive bomber. *(NARA)*.

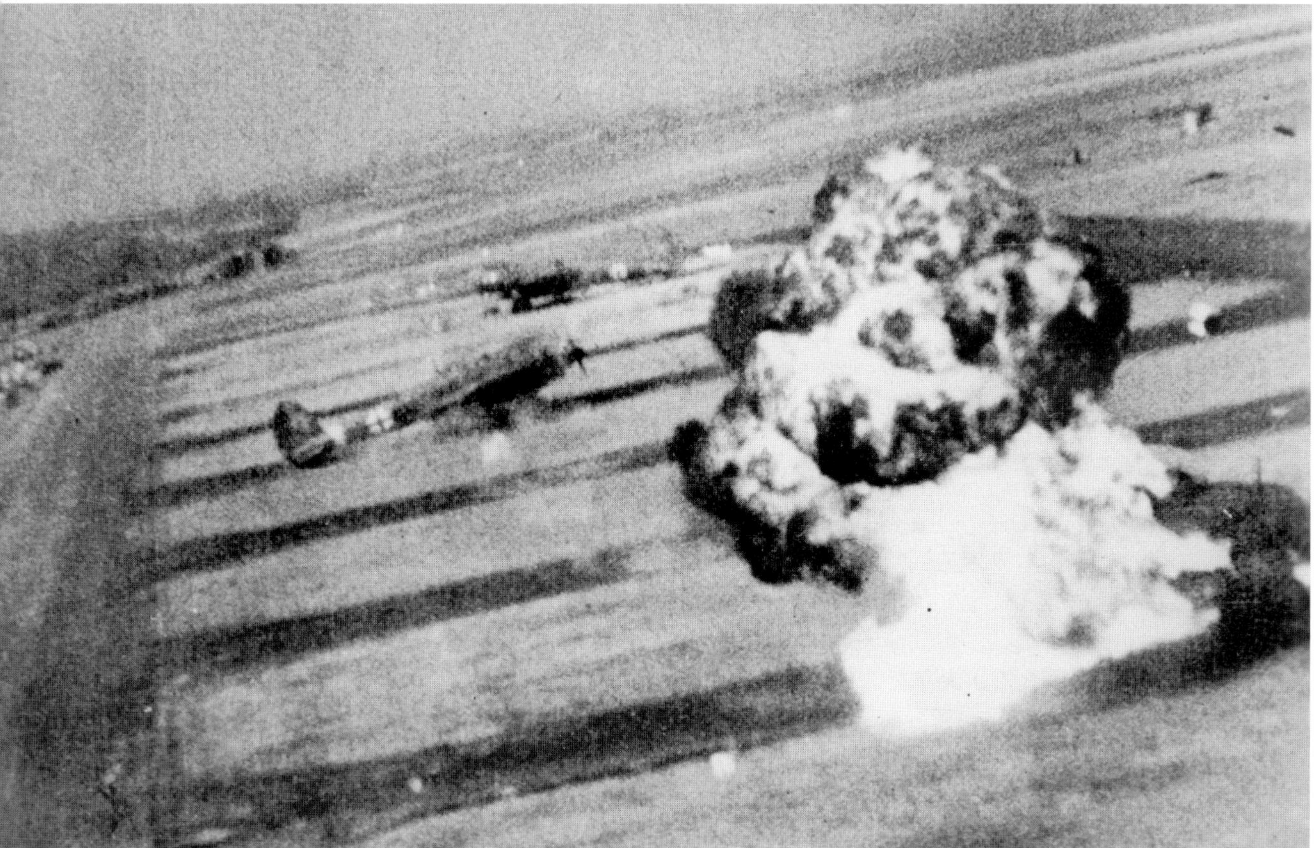

(**Above**) A German Focke-Wulf (Fw) 190 single-seat fighter is shown disabled alongside a bomb crater at Biscari Airfield that was attacked before the amphibious assaults. The Biscari Airfield was located between other Axis air bases, with Ponte Olivo to the west and Comiso to the east just inland from the Gulf of Gela invasion beaches at Gela and Scoglitti. During the summer of 1943, the Fw 190A-4 was in service. It was fast at over 380 miles per hour at maximal speed and had four 20mm fixed forward-firing cannon in the leading edges of the wing along with two 7.92mm fixed forward-firing machine-guns in the upper part of the forward fuselage enabling it to be excellent ground-attack and anti-shipping strafing aircraft. *(NARA)*

(**Opposite, above**) A wrecked Axis hangar along with the rear assembly and fuselage of a German fighter are shown amid the ruins after an Allied bombing raid on one of the five major airfields in the Gerbini complex in the north-western area of the Plain of Catania. This marshy area of Sicilian flatland also housed over a dozen satellite airfields. In all, the Axis had 19 main airfields on Sicily, which were mostly destroyed or abandoned at the time of the Allied amphibious assault. A twin-engine *Luftwaffe* Ju-88 medium bomber, suggested by its shape and insignia, is shown deserted in the background. *(NARA)*

(**Opposite, below**) Rail depots and yards were also targeted by the Allied Air Forces to destroy the integrity of an Axis aerial response to the invasion. Here, the ruined hulks of *Luftwaffe* fighters are shown in proximity to disabled railcars carrying the fuselages of larger aircraft at Erice Napola, located on the north-western tip of Sicily in Trapani Province, on 25 July 1943. Such continued devastation after the invasion contributed to the Italian king asking for Mussolini's resignation on this day. *(NARA)*

A British-crewed M4A1 'Sherman' tank is seen moving through a Roman-designed arch with a medieval tower in the background in the Sicilian town of Cassabile located on the coast in the Gulf of Noto between Avola to the south and Syracuse to the north. British Commandos and elements of the British 5th Infantry Division assaulted this locale during the early days following the Eighth Army's amphibious landings. *(NARA)*

(**Opposite, above**) An American amphibious 2½-ton payload capacity truck, the DUKW, loaded with aviation gasoline and ammunitions is situated next to a single-seat Curtiss P-40 Warhawk fighter-bomber at a captured Axis airfield on Sicily as it is fuelled and loaded for a combat sortie. According to the US Army Transportation Museum, the acronym DUKW denoted a number of properties. First, the 'D' identified it as a vehicle designed in 1942. The 'U' categorised its 'utility' 2½-ton amphibious truck purpose. The 'K' indicated a front-wheel drive and the 'W' conveyed its rear-wheel drive. Other explanations for the DUKW acronym also exist. The P-40 had a maximal speed of 340 miles per hour and was armed with six 0.5in fixed forward-firing machine-guns in the leading edges of the wings. It could also be external fit with a 1500lb bomb load adding to its ground attack capability against enemy ground positions. *(NARA)*

(**Opposite, below**) British Royal Navy personnel are seen inspecting Italian railway cars damaged during the Allied bombardment with intact 102/35mm pedestal-mounted coastal guns that were abandoned by the enemy at the Italian Navy stronghold at Syracuse on 10 July 1943. In the Syracuse-Augusta area, the Italian Navy utilised artillery trains for mobile coastal defence between the two ports on Sicily's eastern coast. *(NARA)*

(**Above**) A panoramic view of the terrain around Enna in Central Sicily is demonstrated. This was the site of intense combat between both US Seventh Army and British Eighth Army troops clashing with the *Wehrmacht*'s 15th Panzer-grenadier Division. As shown, rudimentary tree-lined roads, typical for inland Sicily, lead to hilly terrain upon which the Sicilians had built their towns and small cities. *(USAMHI)*

(**Opposite, above**) American soldiers of the 47th Infantry Regiment are shown casually marching along a typical Sicilian minor dirt-covered roadway. This regiment was part of the US 9th Infantry Division, which had landed in Algeria in north-west Africa in November 1942. The GIs are marching towards Messina and get their initial glimpse of Mount Etna in the distance. The Caronie Mountains were the highest and most rugged mountains of the island with peaks from 4,500 to 5,400 feet leading south-eastwards into Mount Etna itself, which was 10,000 feet high and 20 miles in diameter at the base. The Caronie Mountain chain ran from the vicinity of Troina, in Central Sicily, almost to Messina. Just to the west of the Caronie Mountains were the equally rugged Madonie Mountains. These topographic features would divide the American forces advancing through Central Sicily and along the northern coast into essentially two mutually exclusive campaigns. Terrain such as this was to be a 'force multiplier' for the Axis and delayed the American advance to Messina. Major-General Manton Eddy's division arrived from North Africa at Palermo on 1 August 1943. The division reassembled at Nicosia on 4 August and replaced the 1st Infantry Division three days later as well as relieving elements of the US 45th Infantry and 82nd Airborne Divisions. General Patton utilised these infantrymen for the eastward push to first Randazzo and then onto Messina through this mountainous terrain of north-eastern Sicily, which would be a hindrance to the US 2nd Armoured Division. *(NARA)*

(**Opposite, below**) A panoramic view of the Plain of Catania is depicted above. This topographical area was the scene of some of the harshest fighting between the British Eighth Army and the Axis forces. The Plain of Catania was the only suitable flat land on the east coast for the airbases at Gerbini that had to be captured by the Allies to provide tactical air support for their advance onto Messina. In the foreground is the town of Lentini at the southern end of the Plain of Catania, which was captured by the Eighth Army on 17 July 1943. Malaria was a notable feature of the Catania Plain and the British troops in this area were soon ordered to take a mepecrine tablet daily and to roll their sleeves down and wear long trousers after dark. This was not always feasible and malaria broke out soon after the landings in addition to the tenacious fight for this area. *(NARA)*

American soldiers of the 30th Infantry Regiment of Major-General Lucian Truscott's 3rd Division are shown cautiously moving around a Cape Calava cliff, along Sicily's mountainous northern coast where the roadbed had been blown out by the retreating Germans. To continue the American advance onto Messina, the US 10th Engineer Battalion began the construction task of erecting a 'Bridge Hung in the Sky', with Truscott being the first to cross the spanned gap in a Jeep. *(NARA)*

(**Opposite, above**) Company A of the 16th Infantry Regiment, US 1st Division is shown moving onwards to Troina, the highest situated town in Sicily. The battle for Troina, which pitted the US 1st Infantry Division against the defensive works of the German 15th Panzergrenadier Division, was one of the most costly fights for American forces during the thirty-eight-day Sicilian campaign. The Axis forces were deeply entrenched in the hills that both dominated the approaches to the town and were difficult to outflank. In addition, the barren landscape below the town offered almost no cover for the advancing American infantry, making them easy targets for the Axis gunners situated above them. *(NARA)*

(**Opposite, below**) An aerial view from atop Troina is shown. This central Sicilian mountaintop town overlooked the valley below. The near-exhausted US 1st Infantry Division, which had landed at Gela on 10 July 1943 along with the 39th Infantry Regiment of the US 9th Division attached to it, pushed its way eastward against stiffening German opposition and captured Nicosia on 28 July. Then the GIs moved further eastward to Troina, which constituted one of the main anchors of the Etna Line and was defended by the German 15th Panzergrenadier Division and elements of the Italian Aosta Division. *(USAMHI)*

A US Army half-track is shown moving through a narrow street of the Central Sicilian town of Nicosia. This town had been essentially built on a mountaintop and was situated to the west of Troina. Elements of the US 1st Infantry Division captured Nicosia prior to its continued eastward movement along Highway 120 to its bitter battle for Troina. *(NARA)*

(**Opposite, above**) An aerial view of the beach near Licata that was assaulted by the US 3rd Infantry Division on 10 July 1943 is shown. A Landing Craft, Infantry (LCI), in the centre of the photograph was able to get almost up to the shoreline as there were no prominent sandbars at this assault beach at the western end of the Gulf of Gela on Sicily's southern shore. To the left of the LCI are smaller landing craft, which brought in more infantry and some smaller vehicles and towed artillery pieces as evidenced by the tracks in the sand above the shoreline. Once captured, the Allies wanted to utilise Licata as a small port. *(NARA)*

(**Opposite, below**) Landing Craft, Tanks (LCTs) are shown moving close to the sand at the assault beach near Licata on Sicily's southern coast. Major-General Lucian Truscott's 3rd Division, with an attached Combat Command A of the US 2nd Second Armoured Division and a unit of Moroccan Goums, had approximately 45,000 troops to capture this objective. Licata, a city and minor port with a population of 30,000 Sicilians, also had road and rail facilities and was situated along a plain that rises to a dome-shaped plateau of 500 feet in height about 5 miles from the city. A Sicilian coastal road (Highway 115), located near the mouth of the Salso River 3 miles to the north-west of the port, connected Licata to Highway 122, which ran south-west to north-east and linked Porto Empedocle-Agrigento-Canicatti-Caltanissetta-Enna. After seizing Licata and opening it up as a minor port facility, Truscott was to move his infantry and support armour north-west to Palma di Montechiaro and Campobello, the latter south of Canicatti. As is evident in the above photograph, within a short distance from the shoreline the beachhead quickly became farmland situated on rolling hills. Smoke is seen billowing from some buildings off in the distance, which probably housed some Axis guns that were bombarded by Allied planes and naval gunfire. The American landings faced significantly more resistance than the British faced at their landing beaches on Sicily's eastern coast. *(NARA)*

20

(**Above**) An aerial view is shown of the American amphibious landing at the beach near Scoglitti, on Sicily's southern coast to the east of Gela at the other end of the Gulf of Gela. The US 45th Infantry Division made the assault at Scoglitti against light opposition. However, the rough seas of the night before the sunny bright D-Day had created some havoc for the amphibious force. The 45th Division's 180th Infantry Regiment had been scattered over a 10-mile front due to the surf conditions. In addition, 150–200 Allied landing craft had become stranded on the shoreline. The conditions in the Mediterranean Sea proved more challenging to the Americans than the Italian defenders at this beachhead. Scoglitti's beach area was composed of soft sand, which gradually rose to 40–80-foot dunes. Pillboxes were scattered along the beaches, the dune line and the inland highways. A few coastal artillery batteries were also situated in this area. *(NARA)*

(**Opposite, above**) An aerial view of the Gela locale with its town, beach area and the Plain of Gela inland from the beach. Like Licata, the Allies wanted to use Gela as a minor port. However, until occupied, beach maintenance for the unloading of supplies would be a time-consuming necessity for the US 1st Infantry Division. Although the beaches in the Gulf of Gela appeared ideal for amphibious operations, shifting sandbars covered by insufficient amounts of water to float larger landing craft carrying vehicles and heavy equipment were numerous, especially at Gela. This would delay unloading at Gela considerably and the nearby transports and landing craft would provide an inviting target for Axis aerial assault. The Plain of Gela would also allow the Axis to mount armoured counter-attacks on 10 and 11 July at the slowly-developing Gela beachhead. *(USAMHI)*

(**Opposite, below**) The American light cruiser, the USS *Boise*, is seen crossing the bow of LST 325 to fire a salvo at Axis positions at Gela. In this manner, naval gunfire not only destroyed or disabled fixed Axis positions inland, but was capable of interdicting German Panzer movement across the Plain of Gela and Italian infantry counter-attacks towards the US 1st Infantry Division's slowly developing beachhead. *(USAMHI)*

#2

(**Above**) The proximity of the Plain of Gela (*background*), onto which the Axis was to launch repeated armoured counter-attacks, to the offshore American warships enabled heavy naval gunfire to interrupt the movement of Nazi Mk III and Mk IV Panzers toward the US 1st Infantry Division's beachhead. The shallow plains behind the assault beaches extended inland only a few miles before merging with the foothills of the southern Sicilian plateau beyond. As shown, salvos from US warships just offshore exploded on the Plain of Gela with devastating effect on the enemy armour traversing it. *(NARA)*

(**Opposite, above**) A wrecked German Mk IV tank of the Hermann Göring Panzer Division is shown shattered in the foreground while at least two others were disabled and abandoned in the background on the Plain of Gela. These tanks were destroyed by accurate US naval gunfire from warships offshore of Gela on 11 July 1943, when the Axis attempted a counter-attack against the US 1st Infantry Division beachhead at Gela. The Panzer Mk IV was identified by its eight bogey wheels. The tank started production in 1934 and continued throughout the war, with the reliable chassis being used for a number of German armoured vehicle variants. The Mk IV Panzer's main 75mm turret gun had long- and short-barrelled models. *(NARA)*

(**Opposite, below**) An Italian coastal defence battery, comprising two Vickers 15in naval guns, attempted to resist the approach of British warships to cover the landing of Montgomery's forces on 10 July 1943 in the vicinity of the Augusta-Syracuse Naval Base area south of Syracuse. *(NARA)*

321307

SIGNAL CORPS
184279

(**Opposite, above**) An Italian Cannone Ansaldo 152/45 S. 1911 G10 coastal gun, deployed to resist amphibious invasion at Palermo, on Sicily's northern shore, which Patton's forces captured in a landward thrust from the south. *(NARA)*

(**Opposite, below**) An Italian concrete pillbox housing a 75mm field-gun had a commanding field of fire view over a road and bridge near Montallegro near Agrigento along Sicily's southern coast to the north-west of Licata. It was Major-General Geoffrey Keyes, the US Seventh Army's deputy commander, who approved a 'reconnaissance in force', only a few days after securing the Licata beachhead, by elements of Truscott's 7th Infantry Regiment in battalion-strength toward Agrigento, which would have far-reaching strategic implications for the revised utilisation of Patton's troops during the campaign. *(NARA)*

(**Above**) An Italian machine-gun is situated in a camouflaged partial concrete enclosure at the Scoglitti beachhead to the far right of American landing zone in the Gulf of Gela. Major-General Troy Middleton's 45th Infantry Division was to land near the fishing village of Scoglitti. Just inland to the shoreline, a broad, relatively open plain unfolded to the foothills of the mountainous terrain and to inland towns perched relatively high. About 10 miles inland of the shore were the 45th Division's main targets, Biscari and Comiso, towns that each had airfields 3 miles to the north of them. Elements of Middleton's Division, the far right flank of US II Corps under Lieutenant-General Omar Bradley, were to also make contact with the 1st Canadian Division at Ragusa, east of Comiso and inland from the Eighth Army's landing sites on the south-eastern tip of Sicily. *(NARA)*

A destroyed Italian armoured vehicle, a captured French Renault R-35 infantry tank of Mobile Group E, is shown in ruins on a Gela street in front of some houses after the American landings on 10 July 1943. Elements of this Axis motorised unit attacked Gela down Highway 117 late on the morning of D-Day. The Renault R-35 was a light tank of which France built 1,600 by 1940. It was France's most numerous tank in service at the time of the Nazi invasion in May 1940. It had a crew of two and only 40mm of armour. Structurally, it was no match for the German Panzers, as it was unable to penetrate even lightly armoured enemy vehicles with its 37mm turret gun, while tactically it was deployed in inadequate numbers to support infantry rather than mount an armoured counter-attack. Many were abandoned during the French retreat of May-June 1940 and Italy claimed several of them as war booty after Mussolini entered the conflict just before the armistice with the new Pétain collaborationist regime. At Gela, these enemy tanks confronted Colonel William O. Darby's 1st and 4th Ranger Battalions along with some American Combat Engineers. Implementing the engineers' bazookas and some American low-calibre AT guns, Darby's unit destroyed some Axis tanks and sent the Italians reeling back along Highway 117. *(NARA)*

A camouflaged Italian AT gun pit situated at the Gela assault beaches is shown. This AT gun was another type of weapon confiscated by the Italians from one of their adversaries, the Yugoslavian Army, in 1941. The AT gun was a Czechoslovakian Skoda-manufactured 47mm weapon. The GI to the right is seen holding one of the gun's 47mm armour-piercing rounds. *(NARA)*

Infantrymen of the Princess Patricia Canadian Light Infantry (PPCLI) are seen making their way through a barbed-wire fence to continue patrolling across an open field as they exit from a grove of fruit trees. Soon after consolidating their amphibious landing against only cursory opposition from Italian coastal defenders that were both ill-equipped and ill-trained, the 1st Canadian Division exited from their beachhead, at the extreme east of Sicily's southern coast in the vicinity of Pachino. The Canadian 1st Infantry Division was to advance north-westerly beginning on 13 July 1943 towards Vizzini, first, and then onto Caltagirone. Both of these Sicilian locales were situated on a road that had previously been assigned within the US 45th Infantry Division's zone of operations. Vizzini, at the junction of three major roads and being at 2,000ft above sea level, was typical of the towns in the mountains of Sicily, which were built there to create a fortress for defence against invaders that the Nazis would utilise to their utmost advantage. Before getting to the highway, due north of the beachhead, the Canadians would need to cross an inland coastal plain between Noto to the east and Ragusa to the west. *(NARA)*

(**Above, left**) Axis landmines and booby traps were numerous and were to both delay the Allied advance and inflict demoralising casualties as the inland advance proceeded. Above is an example of a German AT Tellermine, which was to detonate under 350lb pressure. It was 12in in width and 3in in height. To the left of the carrying handle is a screw cap protruding from the landmine's top. *Teller* is German for dish or plate, which accurately describes the shape of this landmine. Because of its rather high operating pressure to set off the fuse, only a vehicle or heavy object passing over the mine would set it off. The Tellermine was capable of blasting the tracks off any Allied tank or destroying a lightly armoured vehicle. Over 3 million Tellermines were produced by Germany from 1943–1944. Some were improvised to contain a booby trap or anti-handling device inside the mine. Any attempt to disarm the mine by unscrewing the pressure plate or the screw cap in order to remove the fuse would automatically detonate the device. *(NARA)*

(**Above, right**) A German light Panzer mine. This explosive device could be used against very lightly armoured vehicles, such as motorcycles, Jeeps, a Universal Carrier or as an anti-personnel weapon. It was 10in wide and 3in in height and could be set at varied pressures for detonation. *(NARA)*

(**Right**) A German 'S' (*Schrapnellmine*) mine or 'Bouncing Betty'. When detonated, this device rose to about 5ft in the air and exploded sending steel-ball shrapnel flying in all directions to inflict casualties on unshielded Allied infantrymen in their upper torso and head regions. These devices were 5in in height and weighed about 9lb, containing over 6oz of explosive charge. This variant had a double tripwire detonating mechanism, which would be at an infantryman's foot level. The standard pressure sensor was activated by approximately 15lb or greater of weight, so that animals or debris would not prematurely detonate it. By the war's end, the Germans had manufactured almost 2,000,000 of these explosive devices. *(NARA)*

A planted or installed German 'S' (*Schrapnellmine*) mine or 'Bouncing Betty' with a three-pronged wire detonator attached to a tripwire at ground level. As is evident, when camouflaged this device might be difficult to visualise from 5 to 6ft above it. However, the 'S' mine was constructed mostly of metal, so it could easily be detected by metal detectors, which were not usually available to typical infantry patrols moving cross-country or single-file columns moving along a road or roadside. These 'S' mines, when discovered with careful bayonet probing, could usually be disarmed. (*NARA*)

Many Allied soldiers were either wounded or killed by Axis booby traps. Here, a GI has been killed as a pair of US engineers searched for metallic mines with a SCR-625 mine detector in the rubble surrounding his corpse. It would not have been unusual for the enemy to have planted a mine in proximity to a dead or wounded comrade as a lure to inflict additional casualties. Ironically, the dead US soldier was lying under a sign in Italian that extolled the virtues of fascism and proclaimed, 'We will win!'. *(NARA)*

(**Opposite, above**) Two American engineers using their bayonets in a customary patrolling method to first discover and then carefully dig up a German Tellermine that had been sown on a Sicilian road, as this was to disable or destroy an armoured vehicle. This process was time-consuming. However, metal detectors were not always available. Careful manual probing of the soil with a bayonet at a low angle that would not accidentally depress the pressure sensor was required for this manoeuvre. *(NARA)*

(**Opposite, below**) A pair of US Army Engineers are seen searching for metallic mines in the ruins of Troina in Central Sicily, which took the US 1st Infantry Division five days to capture from a tenacious German defence. The engineer on the right was holding the SCR-625 mine detector while the kneeling one on the left probed the ground carefully with his bayonet where a metal object was detected. The SCR-625 operator carried a battery and electronic pack on his right side. The mine detector consisted of a 6ft pole, at the end of which is attached an 18in diameter wooden disc with a cylindrical search coil underneath. This device was able to detect metal mines up to a foot below the surface of the soil. It weighed approximately 8lb. The SCR-625 mine detector made its combat debut in North Africa after the Operation *Torch* landings. On Sicily, as compared to North Africa, both the different soil composition and German advances in constructing mines of wood or plastic to avoid metal detection, made the job of the sappers very difficult and time consuming. *(NARA)*

(**Above**) Enemy mines were also injurious to Axis troops if they were unaware about their location. In the above photograph, American medics tended to one of their wounded officers when a US Jeep struck a Tellermine in the background. Dead Italian soldiers are seen lying in the foreground, having been thrown from their truck, which was destroyed after it went over another one of their own Axis mines. *(NARA)*

(**Opposite, above**) A German pillbox housing a machine-gun at an inland location to blend in with the terrain. It was partially built of bomb casings and stones and then covered with vegetation that blended in with the surrounding flora, on all sides except at the aperture. *(NARA)*

(**Opposite, below**) The front of an Italian pillbox at the base of a jetty in Porto Empedocle is shown blending in well with the surrounding landscape of the port. Often there was a rifle pit and trench at the rear of a pillbox. The Sicilian port city was heavily shelled by the US Navy cruiser *Philadelphia*. Agrigento and Porto Empedocle were captured by the US 3rd Division and Ranger Battalions, respectively, on 16 July 1943. With Agrigento in Allied hands, Patton intended to further move on towards the capture of Palermo, the capital of Sicily, on the island's northern coast. Although the battles for these two southern Sicilian cities were brief, over 6,000 Italians were captured along with tanks, artillery and vehicles. *(NARA)*

(**Above**) An inland German pillbox situated on an undulating hilltop is very well-camouflaged with netting and hay piled on all of its sides. A communication trench exited the back of the structure. The placement of this pillbox gave its previous enemy occupants an excellent field of fire on advancing Allied troops in the valley region below it. After its capture, an American serviceman is seen making some notes about the defensive work. *(NARA)*

(**Opposite, above**) Axis pillboxes with a 75mm M1897 field-gun at Ponte Dirillo overlooking the Acate (or Dirillo) River 15 miles north-east of Gela are shown. The Acate is a 34-mile long river that springs from the Hyblaean Mountains and flows into the Gulf of Gela. These enemy fortifications were in the vicinity of Biazza Ridge, which was assaulted by elements of the 505th Parachute Infantry Regiment (PIR), led by Colonel James Gavin, on 11 July 1943. Just to the north-west of this site was the Axis airfield at Ponte Olivo. The other airfields targeted for capture at Biscari and Comiso were located due north and east of these fortified positions. *(NARA)*

(**Opposite, below**) An Axis pillbox with barbed-wire, netting and some camouflage around its outside structure is shown. This fortification was located between Gela and Licata. The Gulf of Gela is seen in the background with the pillbox commanding the coastal plain located to the front and right of the defensive structure. Many of these pillboxes were manned by poorly trained Italian troops with low morale, and they received heavy naval gunfire and aerial attack prior to and during the invasion. *(NARA)*

(**Above**) An Axis pillbox is shown in ruins at San Croce Camerina, a coastal area in Ragusa Province, south of Comiso on Sicily's southern coast near the junction of the US 157th Infantry Regiment, 45th Division and the Canadian 1st Infantry Division's landing beaches. Many paratroopers from the 505th Parachute Infantry Regiment (PIR) landed inadvertently in this Eighth Army sector, near San Croce Camerina, between midnight and 0100 hrs on 10 July 43. On D-Day, the two American forces, comprising the 1st Battalion, 157th Infantry Regiment, US 45th Division and most of the paratroopers from the 2nd Battalion, 505th PIR, coincidently attacked the town of San Croce Camerina. An infantry company drove eastwards onto Ragusa and entered the town by early evening after making the Italian garrison at San Croce Camerina prisoners within hours of the landings. The Americans also occupied Hill 643 overlooking the Comiso airfield. *(USAMHI)*

(**Opposite, above**) A Sicilian house-front in Gela had a prepared machine-gun position, indicated by the plaster to the building's lower façade. Heavy street fighting occurred in Gela as the Italians counter-attacked there with a motorised group comprising infantry, motorcycle, and artillery companies and some French R-35 Renault tanks acquired as captured war *matériel* in June 1940. Colonel Darby's Force X, consisting of elements of the 1st and 4th Rangers along with some combat engineers, broke up the attack. *(USAMHI)*

(**Opposite, below**) A view of a Gela street from a Sicilian home's interior, in which a portion of the outside wall had been excised to permit the Italian defenders to place some of their automatic weapons and light anti-tank artillery for firing on any Allied assault troops. *(NARA)*

(**Above**) Soldiers of the Canadian Royal Army Service Corps are shown riding their mules with a Universal Carrier following them to bring supplies such as water, food and ammunition to front-line troops situated in difficult positions for supply vehicles to reach. Many of the mule riders and handlers had previously been cowboys from Canada's western provinces, such as Alberta. *(NARA)*

(**Opposite page**) Sergeant H.E. Cooper of the 48th Highlanders of Canada is shown posing with his beard and netting. Both the facial hair and the netting covering the head were useful in combating the mosquitos in the wet terrain of eastern Sicily, especially within the Plain of Catania, which proved to be a rugged battleground for Montgomery's forces to win from the Germans in order to obtain possession of the Gerbini complex of airfields. It was not only the mosquito infestation and consequent malaria that afflicted these troops, but the intense summer climate and open terrain, which provided little shade from the sun on the island. Men of the 1st Canadian Infantry Division were fighting their first campaign in Sicily after spending months to years in the United Kingdom training. The Canadians had not been with Eighth Army in the North African desert. Even Montgomery had noted on 13 July in his diary that the Canadians 'had definitely to be rested; the men were not very fit, and they suffered severely form the hot sun and many got badly burnt'. Although probably an underestimate, during the campaign in Sicily, it was approximated that eighty-three admissions to hospital per 1,000 troops were due to malaria. This mosquito-borne parasitic disease was caused by both the relatively benign *Plasmodium vivax* species and the more malignant *Plasmodium falciparum*. Ironically, to combat the intense Sicilian heat, most Eighth Army soldiers went into action wearing shorts and were often unable to change into long trousers after sundown, when mosquitos were most active. Most training in regards to mosquito control was inadequate, and since the ingestion of anti-malarial drugs was irregular the disease was not seriously prevented initially. Most Eighth Army troops were issued with the old Mark I anti-mosquito cream, which was universally disliked because it was too greasy. Also, adequate numbers of mosquito nets arrived on Sicily too late. There were no quick chemical cures for heat and sun over-exposure. *(NARA)*

An American soldier with a large water container strapped to his back prepares to make the climb up some rocky terrain to get to his thirsty comrades. The summer Mediterranean heat was intense with dehydration a constant threat to troops remote from water sources. *(NARA)*

(**Opposite, above**) Men of the US 30th Infantry Regiment of the 3rd Division, as evidenced by some having their left shoulder patch visible, crowding around a water trough to fill up their canteens and have a cigarette, even though a dog has immersed itself in the water. *(USAMHI)*

(**Opposite, below**) A Canadian infantry section from the Princess Patricia's Canadian Light Infantry (PPCLI), a mechanised infantry unit, attacked the smoking remnants of a German transport column that Canadian artillery had caught in the open in a valley area during their advance Valguarnera, *en route* to Enna in Central Sicily. The PPCLI won its first battle honours of the war for their action at Leonforte, which was directly due north of Valguarnera. *(NARA)*

(**Above**) In order to avoid being bombarded by enemy mortar, artillery or aerial assault, Allied infantry on Sicily learned the value of digging their temporary entrenchment deeply into the soil of the island wherever the terrain permitted. Three Canadian soldiers of the 1st Canadian Infantry Division dug two separate deep foxholes at this site. Due to the rocky composition of the terrain, the soldier in the foreground utilised a pick to achieve depth within his entrenchment. *(NARA)*

(**Opposite, above**) Always seeking the tactical advantage of possessing higher ground, an American soldier of the US 30th Infantry Regiment of the 3rd Division is shown digging a weapon pit for his venerable 0.30in calibre Browning M1917 water-cooled machine-gun on a hill overlooking Brolo, which was situated between Cape Orlando and Cape Calava, after one of Truscott's patented amphibious operations along Sicily's northern coast on 11 August 1943. The gun was already loaded with a belt of ammunition coming from the ammunition can just beneath the barrel. The tube to instil water around the jacket of the barrel was located at the very front end of the machine-gun. The water can was at the back lip of the weapon pit near the soldier's helmet. *(NARA)*

(**Opposite, below**) The Sicilian soil was also used for the unpleasant task of burying one's comrade-in-arms in the field. Here a private of the US 30th Infantry Regiment is shown digging a grave on the face of a hill overlooking the northern coastal town of Brolo on the 3rd Infantry Division's advance towards Messina on 11 August 1943. *(NARA)*

186410

Occupying terrain with some height was not only a sound defensive tactic, it also enabled artillery spotters to both locate enemy movements and to sight where their rounds were falling to call in adjustments to the mortar or artillery batteries. In the above photograph, an American lieutenant serving as an artillery spotter reported back to his battery via field telephone where the rounds were landing below this typical Sicilian country house. GIs behind the stone wall to the left observed the enemy movement below the hill position. *(NARA)*

*(left-to-right)* Lieutenant-Colonel William Wyman, 2nd Lieutenant John Lamb and 1st Lieutenant Walter Hillermeyer of the 7th Field Artillery Battalion manning a US observation post near Cerami. From there they gave co-ordinates to divert artillery-fire onto Troina atop the mountain in the distance to assist the US 1st Infantry Division in their five-day attack on this strategic town tenaciously held by the Germans. *(USAMHI)*

American Colonel Lyle Bernard and his radioman are shown setting up their command post (CP) atop Monte Cipolla, which overlooked Brolo on Sicily's northern coast. Bernard's 2nd Battalion, US 30th Infantry Regiment had made another amphibious operation in its continued drive towards Messina on 11 August 1943. The apprehensive look on Bernard's face reflected that while he was establishing his CP on this steep hill about midway between the Naso and Brolo Rivers, which dominated the coastal highway and the ground to the east and west, he was anxiously awaiting the link-up with other 3rd Infantry Division battalions who were still 10 miles behind them to the west. The northern coast's highway, Route 113, was the German 29th Panzergrenadier Division's main escape route to the east and Bernard's amphibious landing to the rear of the enemy west of Cape Orlando at Brolo was sure to evoke a severe Nazi counter-attack. To relieve Bernard's now isolated battalion, every available element of Truscott's 3rd Infantry Division along with Darby's 3rd Ranger Battalion had to break through the Germans' main line of resistance along the Naso Ridge. The terrain in the landing area near Brolo was dominated by Mount Cipolla, the base of which lies some 450 yards inland from the beach, the top of which reaches an altitude of 750ft. From such heights, Bernard in his CP directed some batteries of self-propelled and towed field artillery as well as naval gunfire from the offshore escorting USS *Philadelphia* and six destroyers. *(NARA)*

Wounded 1st Canadian Division infantrymen near Valguarnera were carried from the battlefield on litters by Royal Canadian Army Medical Corps (RCAMC) stretcher-bearers (SBs) to an area just to the rear. There the Canadian casualties received timely care for their battle wounds by other personnel of the RCAMC in the open before being carried off to a field dressing station with its medical officers. Battle casualties were not the only admissions to Allied field hospitals on Sicily. The failure of anti-malaria efforts on the part of the Allied command led to 11,590 cases of the disease recorded by Eighth Army during the Sicilian campaign as opposed to 7,798 battle casualties admitted to hospital. There were a further 9,892 malaria cases in the US Seventh Army. In fact, an Eighth Army publication, *Crusader*, quipped, 'Since the start of the Sicily campaign, the tiny mosquito had been a more powerful enemy than the German.' Dichlorodiphenyltrichloroethane (DDT), manufactured by the Swiss Geigy Corporation, had undergone testing in the United Kingdom and America in 1942–1943. This insecticide would have a decisive role in the control of malaria during the ensuing Italian Campaign, but not until malaria had wreaked havoc amongst Allied troops in the wet, marshy terrain of the Plain of Catania and elsewhere on Sicily where this disease was endemic. *(NARA)*

An American field hospital functioning outside a Sicilian farmhouse near Cefalù, which was located to the west of Santo Stefano and San Fratello, on the island's northern coast bordering the Tyrrhenian Sea. The field hospital was less than a mild from an airfield, from which C-46 and C-47 transport aircraft would evacuate the severely wounded cases to rear echelon North African hospitals. The GI on the makeshift treatment table is about to get an intravenous infusion of plasma to help resuscitate him from his blood loss from his apparent head wound, which is bandaged. In addition to the life-saving effects of plasma infusions, penicillin was beginning to transform the treatment of wounds and burns. By 1943, large-scale manufacture of penicillin was well under way in the United States and beginning with the Sicilian campaign, it was routinely used in the treatment of war wounds. The plentiful supply of penicillin to the Allied armies constituted one of the chief differences between medical provisions for Allied and German troops. *(NARA)*

WH-1377905

(**Opposite, above**) The inland roadways of Sicily were often very narrow, which severely hampered the movement of Allied motorised units and towed artillery. As shown above, an American reconnaissance Jeep of the 505th Parachute Infantry Regiment (PIR), heading north-westwards from Gela, made contact with the rear end of a disabled German Mk VI 'Tiger' tank and had to wait for bulldozers to re-open the road. *(NARA)*

(**Opposite, below**) A Canadian reconnaissance patrol is shown rounding a turn on a narrow Sicilian road past two German vehicles destroyed by Allied artillery. A Canadian soldier in the middle of the road is shown removing some of the wrecks' debris to enable his fellow soldiers pass in their Jeeps. The German unarmed utility vehicle in the foreground, with its distinctive spare tyre mounted in the front, was the Volkswagen (VW) Kübel, which fulfilled the Nazi planners' main design considerations of lightness, low cost of production and ease of manufacture. By 1944, over 50,000 of these light utility vehicles had been manufactured. *(NARA)*

(**Above**) Mechanized forces of the US Seventh Army competed for space as they travelled in opposite directions along a narrow Sicilian road near Nicosia, located in the mountainous central portion of the island between Enna and Troina. This area of Sicily comprised the Caronie Mountains, and the primitive nature of the roadways coursing along the face of the heights is evident. *(NARA)*

(**Above**) British troops are seen marching along a coastal highway in the foothills of Mount Etna north of the Plain of Catania. It appears the British truck had difficulty in negotiating a 'hairpin' turn along this section of the road. *(NARA)*

(**Opposite, above**) As difficult as it was for infantry to move along the mountain roads of central and northern Sicily, it was even more challenging for motorised units, especially towing heavy artillery pieces. As is shown, an American truck, loaded with artillerymen, courses over a narrow portion of a Sicilian road leading to a bridge that engineers were just working on clearing in order to get it into position to fire on Troina for the five-day US 1st Infantry Division's attack on the Axis fortress town perched atop a mountain in early August 1943. The gun being towed behind the truck was a 155mm M1 cannon, commonly called the 'Long Tom', one of the most important weapons in the US Army's long-range artillery inventory during the Second World War and, interestingly, was based on a French design used in the First World War. From design to implementation into service took over a decade for the US Army. The 'Long Tom's' carriage with its ten wheels, eight on its gun-mount and two on the trail-mount (the latter two not shown here), was specially designed to augment cross-country movement. It had a maximum range of 25,000 yards and fired one 200-pound round per minute. *(NARA)*

(**Opposite, below**) British soldiers of the 51st Highland Division are seen moving along a Sicilian road away from Pachino, on the south-eastern tip of the island, after its capture early after the amphibious landings. The British infantrymen are shown marching beside an M7 'Priest' self-propelled 105mm Howitzer, while to the other side of the dirt roadway, native Sicilians returned to their homes in mule or donkey-drawn carts. The M7 was a modification of the US Army's M3 Medium 'Grant' or 'Lee' tank. The British received many under the Lend-Lease agreement and deployed them first at the Second Battle of El Alamein in October to November 1942. The drawback of the M7 was that the Howitzer was not standard British issue and, as such, required separate supplies of ammunition. The M7 remained in service throughout the entire war and was also versatile as an armoured personnel carrier. *(NARA)*

(**Opposite, above**) M4 'Sherman' Medium tanks of the US 2nd Armoured Division are seen moving along a dusty road on the way to Palermo on Sicily's northern coast. On their trek, these tanks passed an abandoned Axis field-gun. *(NARA)*

(**Opposite, below**) A pair of Canadian M4 'Sherman' Medium tanks of the 1st Canadian Army Tank Brigade advanced along a dust-clogged road in support of British infantry. On D-Day, the Canadians landed on the western side of the Pachino Peninsula with elements of the British 30th Corps landing near Cape Passero on the eastern side of the peninsula. *(NARA)*

(**Above**) Two American soldiers are casually watching as a US M3 half-track ironically squeezes slowly through a narrow passageway in the central Sicilian town of Cerami, as it had a maximum cross-country speed of 40mph. Cerami was 5 miles to the west of Troina and was captured by the US 1st Infantry Division on 31 July 1943, which corresponded to the start of the five-day onslaught for Troina. It was the 39th Infantry Regiment of the 9th Division, which was attached to the 'Big Red One', that moved 2 miles north-east of Cerami to commence the advance on Troina. Both Major-General Terry de la Mesa Allen and Brigadier-General Theodore Roosevelt, the division's commanding and assistant commanding generals, incorrectly predicted a rapid capture of Troina, largely due to underestimates of German troop and artillery strength there. *(NARA)*

A Canadian armour column supporting the 1st Canadian Infantry Division is shown as it moves through the rubble of the mountaintop town of Regalbuto, which was an inland road communications centre, on 3 August 1943. Regalbuto was one of the central Sicilian towns that was pounded into ruins by Allied fighter-bombers. Nonetheless, the Canadians encountered fierce German resistance from enemy paratrooper units there. Their efforts were part of Operation *Hardgate* (24 July to 7 August), which was a combined British-Canadian effort to capture both Regalbuto and Centuripe to the east. If Regalbuto fell to the Canadians, German General Hube feared a premature withdrawal of his forces, which would create an opening for the Allies to move eastwards towards Adrano, the central anchor of his Axis Mount Etna defence line, east of the Simeto River. True to Hube's prediction, after taking Regalbuto, the Canadians advanced to the Troina River, halfway to Adrano, and then, along with the British 78th Infantry Division, established a bridgehead over the Simeto River, in proximity of Adrano and the base of Mount Etna. *(NARA)*

(**Opposite, above**) A Sicilian bridge near Brolo was demolished by retreating Axis forces along the northern coast of the island in early August. Brolo would be the site where Colonel Lyle Bernard would lead his 2nd Battalion/30th Infantry Regiment of the 3rd Division in an amphibious landing behind a German Panzergrenadier regiment's lines. Bernard's objective was nearby Mount Cipolla, which overlooked Brolo and controlled the coastal Route 113 Highway from Cape Orlando to Brolo. The Americans took Mount Cipolla but had to start beating off the first of many German counter-attacks. The nearest 3rd Division units were still miles away, so road and bridge destruction as in the above photograph slowed the relief of Task Force Bernard. It would take salvos from US Navy warships offshore to help break up the enemy counter-attacks. *(NARA)*

(**Opposite, below**) American Engineers of the 10th Engineer Battalion are shown bridging a gap in a mountain road that was blasted by the Germans on 13 August 1943 to delay the advance of the US 30th Infantry Regiment of the 3rd Division on towards Messina. Along the highway, the 30th Infantry had come to a halt when they reached a partially demolished tunnel and road section at Cape Calava. The 10th Engineer Battalion moved up to restore the road section by hanging what has been termed 'a bridge in the sky', which enabled a Jeep carrying the division's commanding general, Lucian Truscott, across a wooden bridge erected eighteen hours after the reconstruction had commenced. *(NARA)*

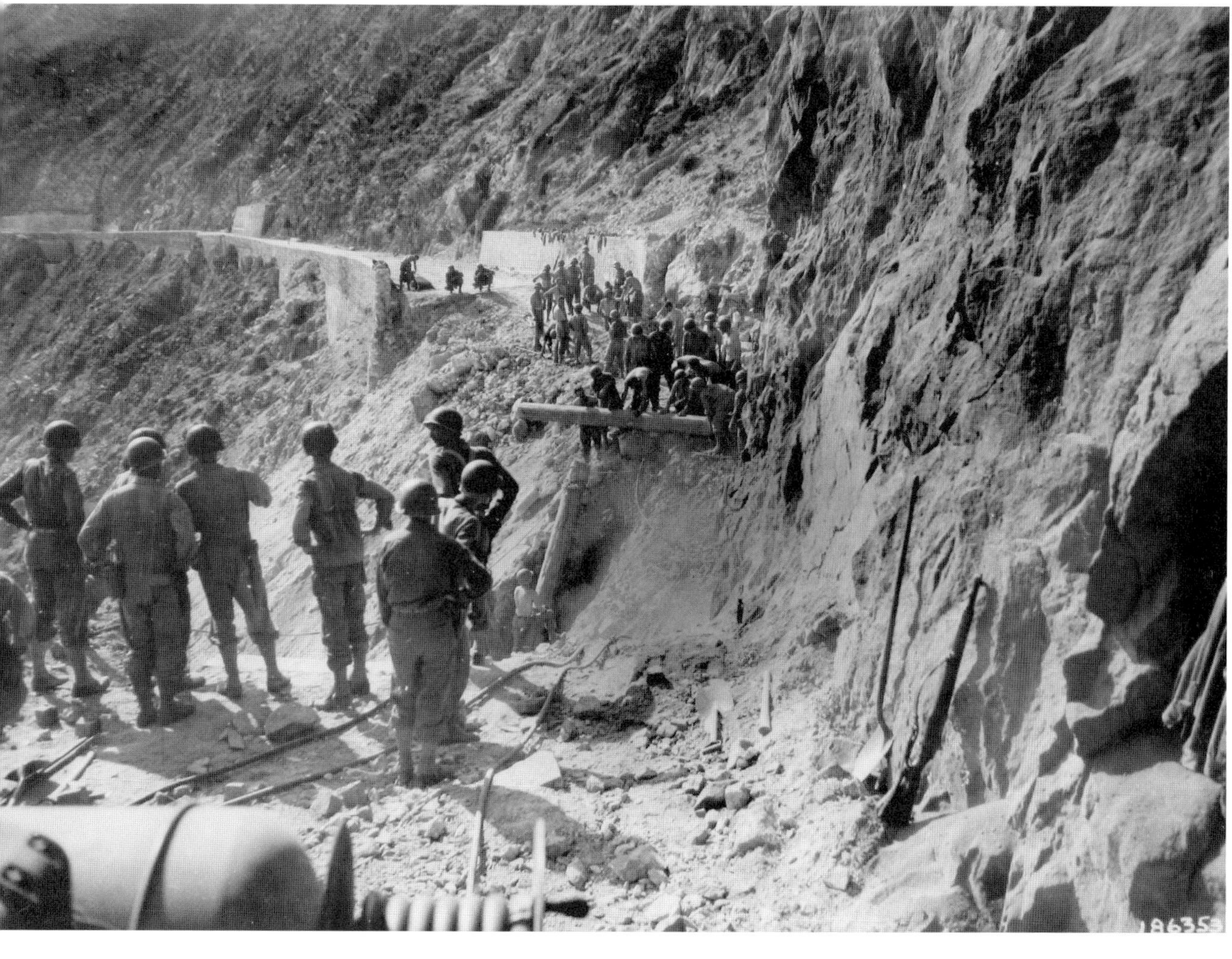

(**Above**) Infantrymen of the 48th Highlanders of Canada are seen marching in a long column out in an open valley along an Italian track on the way towards Adrano at the foot of Mount Etna in early August. The Canadians had captured Regalbuto on 3 August during Operation *Hardgate* (24 July to 7 August 1943). The Canadians would eventually cross the Troina and Simeto rivers on their eastward trek towards Adrano with some of the Caronie Mountains in the far background. *(Author's Collection)*

(**Opposite, above**) Canadian infantrymen marching leisurely through a grove of fruit trees in the vicinity of Nissoria, in Enna Province, during the third week of July 1943. After the Canadian capture of Leonforte, to the north-east of Enna, the flank of the US 1st Infantry Division was secured enabling the Americans to drive north from Enna to Troina. Then the Canadians swung eastwards on an axis Nissoria-Agira-Regalbuto-Adrano during Operation *Hardgate* (24 July to 7 August 1943) to get to the base of Mount Etna from the west, while other British units assaulted northwards along the prominence's eastern side. Nissoria was a sparsely populated village, located in low ground along the highway between low ridges of 2,000 to 3,000ft, which was occupied by the Germans. *(NARA)*

(**Opposite, below**) A band of paratroopers from the US 82nd Airborne Division's 505th Parachute Infantry Regiment moves up through some open Sicilian countryside to a grove of fruit trees inland from the Gela beachhead on D-Day +1, 11 July 1943, near Abbio Priolo. The paratroopers were accompanying company-sized elements of the US 1st Infantry Division who had landed earlier at Gela. These units were proactive in their inland movements before the Axis forces could launch a second day of their counter-attacks as they moved towards against two of their major objectives: the Ponte Olivo airfield and Niscemi. At Abbio Priolo, the 'Big Red One' infantrymen and paratroopers had little time to complete more than hasty weapon pits and shallow foxholes to take on the counter-attack from German Panzers of the Hermann Göring Division. In the absence of Allied naval gunfire or tactical air sorties, the *ad hoc* American force still managed to hold out, using their few bazookas, part of the 16th Infantry Regiment's anti-tank (AT) company, and supported by recently-landed Howitzers of the 7th Field Artillery Battalion. *(USAMHI)*

(**Opposite, above**) British infantrymen racing across an open area, in the face of enemy fire, to storm a disabled German 88 Flak anti-tank/anti-aircraft gun inland from their beachhead within the Gulf of Noto along the south-eastern coast of Sicily. *(NARA)*

(**Opposite, below**) As Allied infantry approached Sicilian towns, they had to be vigilant for enemy positions lurking in buildings and behind stone wall. As shown above, three Americans from a reconnaissance patrol carefully utilise the cover of a stone wall and staircase. One of the infantrymen crouched against the wall while the observer used his binoculars to get a better glimpse of any enemy positions ahead. The third soldier moved forward in a crouched stance, holding his M1 Garand semi-automatic rifle. *(NARA)*

(**Above**) British infantrymen charging across a path between several foot-high stone walls to either side of them as they ferret out enemy sniper positions in the outskirts of Augusta after advancing north along Sicily's eastern coast from the Eighth landings in the Gulf of Noto to the south. *(NARA)*

(**Opposite, above**) American soldiers acted as an advancing edge of an armoured infantry regiment in a sunken lane. There they fired at and took cover from enemy snipers hidden in a tree line off in the distance. These rudimentary roads had been used by Sicilians with their donkey- and mule-drawn carts for centuries. *(NARA)*

(**Opposite, below**) British Eighth Army infantrymen charging forward in a railway station past a dead Italian soldier lying beneath a railcar to the far left. Other infantrymen used the cover of a rail depot building to the right and a boxcar in the background of the photograph from gunfire from entrenched Italian positions. *(NARA)*

(**Above**) An American soldier with his M1 Garand semi-automatic rifle at the ready inspecting destroyed Italian boxcars for any hiding snipers in the Castelbuono railway station and rail depot in the province of Palermo on Sicily's northern coast, which was destroyed by Allied fighter-bomber sorties and artillery shelling. *(NARA)*

(**Opposite page**) House-to-house fighting was not uncommon for the Allied soldiers as they rooted out enemy forces either in hiding or having sequestered themselves in homes and buildings as snipers. Early clashes between elements of the British 5th Infantry Division approaching the outskirts of Syracuse and Axis forces, reinforced by German paratroopers who had been air-landed at Catania, began on the morning of 11 July 1943. The British were eager to quickly secure the ports of Syracuse and Augusta for the unloading of supplies and vehicles for the northerly advance, but it was not until the afternoon of 12 July that Italian coastal batteries in Augusta surrendered, thereby enabling Royal Navy ships to enter Augusta Harbour. In the above photograph, British infantrymen are seen storming through a damaged building in search of the enemy in Augusta. Although the port of Augusta was in British hands by midday on 12 July 1943, the clearing out of snipers took another day. Soon it was evident to soldiers in the Eighth Army that their advance up the east was going to be a contested one all the way. *(NARA)*

(**Above**) Although the British 13th Corps had taken Augusta on 12 July 1943, Catania did not fall until 5 August. As shown above, a section of British infantry advances through the rubble of heavily-defended Catania, which was subjected to intense Allied aerial bombing, artillery shelling and naval gunfire. Many reasons existed for the delay in capturing Catania. However, it was essentially due to an inability to properly deploy British troop formations because of a narrow axis of advance. Therefore, no major opportunity developed to outflank the Axis defenders, comprised of elements of the Hermann Göring Division who withdrew from the city on the night of 4 August. *(NARA)*

By 17 July 1943, Montgomery had written-off a breakthrough at Catania. He would continue to use his 13th Corps to pin down Axis formations in the port city, while the Canadian 1st Infantry Division of 30th Corps would be utilised for a thrust to capture Leonforte first and then move east through the Simeto River valley to Adrano on the western side of Mount Etna. This manoeuvre would, in effect, drive a wedge between the Nazi 15th Panzergrenadier and Hermann Göring Divisions comprising the defence of the Axis Etna Line. By seizing the key road centre of Adrano, Montgomery hoped to cut off the Germans in the Plain of Catania. In the above photograph, Canadian infantrymen storm over piles of rubble in Leonforte, which was tenaciously defended by elements of the 104th Panzergrenadier Regiment, delaying their entry into the central Sicilian town until 22 July, which had preserved the western end of the Axis Etna Line, when the Germans were forced to withdraw. The cost to the Canadian 1st Infantry Division was 275 casualties, mostly in the streets of Leonforte. *(NARA)*

An American soldier of the US 1st Infantry Division is seen searching for enemy snipers in the ruined buildings of Troina in the wake of five days of brutal combat to take the central Sicilian mountain-top town on Highway 120. The first attack by the 39th Infantry Regiment (commanded by Colonel 'Paddy' Flint) of the 45th Division, which was temporarily attached to the 'Big Red One', to bolster it with three additional infantry and one artillery battalions, commenced on 1 August 1943, but it was thrown back after sustaining heavy casualties. Subsequent attacks over the next two days also met with fierce German resistance and high American casualties. An attack on 4 August, stiffened by artillery-fire from numerous battalions' batteries and frequent fighter-bomber sorties, failed to force the Germans to retreat. The town was taken on 6 August by the 1st Infantry Division after 'the worst six days of fighting since Gela'. After the fighting, Generals Allen and Roosevelt were re-assigned, amid some controversy, and Major-General Clarence Huebner took over the division as it was pulled out of the line for a well-earned rest. *(NARA)*

An American M3 75mm Gun Mounted Carriage (GMC) is shown above. This self-propelled gun (SPG) provided close support for the 1st Infantry Division's capture of Troina in the rugged mountainous terrain of central Sicily in early August 1943. Although the 75mm gun was of First World War vintage, utilising the French M1897 design, this SPG had been the primary American heavy tank destroyer fighting German Panzers in Tunisia before the emergence of the M10 tank destroyer, which arrived in March 1943. The M3 75mm GMC was a hasty improvement over its predecessor, the M6 37mm GMC, although the former weapon still suffered from a very limited traverse and its cross-country speed was deemed inadequate. *(NARA)*

The mountainous terrain of central Sicily with conical hills and deep ravines is depicted in the background as Canadian mortar men unload ordnance from their truck for the attack on Leonforte, a town of 22,000 to the north-east of Enna astride Highway 117, the main road to the north coast of the island. The town was built on a steep hillside with its narrow twisty streets giving the enemy a perfect defence for both concealment and street fighting. This town was on the west-to-east axis of Leonforte-Nissoria-Agira-Regalbuto-Adrano on Highway 121, which was to constitute the Eighth Army's 30th Corps shift to the north that would serve as a prelude to Operation *Hardgate* from 24 July to 7 August 1943. On 17 July, 30th Corps received orders to bypass Enna and swing north for an advance on Leonforte. General Bradley notified General Leese, the 30th Corps commander, that the US II Corps would take Enna. This was to be Montgomery's new push for Messina as his 13th Corps had been stalemated in their drive for Catania on the narrow coastal corridor on the eastern side of Mount Etna. The Seaforth Highlanders of Canada were initially sent in to attack Leonforte on 20–21 July but the Germans held the town in strength and disrupted the Canadian advance at the ravine near Leonforte, where they called on their mortars and field artillery to provide 'plunging' bombardment on the German positions. On 22 July, the Edmonton Regiment was ordered to take over the attack, which allowed the Seaforth Highlanders to withdraw and reorganise. As the Edmonton Regiment infantry entered the town, they too were counter-attacked by German tanks and the town's enemy defenders, leaving the Canadian infantry isolated in the centre of Leonforte, with house-to-house fighting ongoing. Early the next day, Canadian sappers spanned a bridge across the ravine leading into Leonforte that had been demolished by the enemy, thereby allowing the Princess Patricia Canadian Light Infantry Regiment (PPCLI) supported with four tanks of the Trois-Rivières Regiment and anti-tank guns to race to the Edmontons' rescue. *(NARA)*

(**Opposite page**) Two infantrymen of the Princess Patricia Canadian Light Infantry Regiment (PPCLI) are seen carefully scanning the rooftops of Agira for enemy snipers and hidden machine-gun nests. Each Canadian soldier carried the standard issue Short Magazine Lee-Enfield (SMLE) No.1 Mk III, which was the primary infantry weapon of British and Commonwealth forces during the Second World War. The bolt-action rifle was one of a long-serving series of weapons, with specialised variants still used decades after the war. The SMLE rifle first entered service in 1907 and fired a .303in-calibre cartridge. Its ten-round box magazine was loaded with five-round charger clips. The rifle had a range of over 1,600 feet. Agira was directly between Nissoria to the west and Regalbuto to the east on Route 121 that headed further east to Adrano, the road junction at the western end of Mount Etna. Agira was a furious battle for the Canadians, who sustained almost 500 casualties to take the medieval town in order to move on Regalbuto. As part of the British Eighth Army's 30th Corps front in central Sicily, the Canadian advance would pose a serious threat to the German central anchor of their Etna Line, at Adrano. On a small hill east of the city of Agira is the Canadian War Cemetery with 490 graves. *(NARA)*

(**Above**) A Canadian Bren gunner and accompanying infantryman of the Princess Patricia Canadian Light Infantry Regiment (PPCLI) are seen taking cover while on patrol along Via Pozzillo in Agira at the end of July 1943. After bypassing Enna in order to capture Leonforte, as part of the Eighth Army's 30th Corps advance in central Sicily, the 1st Canadian Infantry Division turned east towards Agira, meeting strong pockets of resistance, mostly from elements of the German 15th Panzergrenadier and Hermann Göring Divisions. The first unit to reach Agira on 19 July was the British 231st Infantry or Malta Brigade, under Brigadier Robert 'Roy' Urquhart (who would have the dubious distinction of commanding the British 1st Airborne Division at Arnhem during Operation *Market Garden* in September 1944), which was attached to the 1st Canadian Division. These Eighth Army troops had marched over 150 miles in the preceding week, during peak Sicilian summer heat. The Canadians mounted their attack on 22–23 July. *(NARA)*

(**Above**) During the 1st Canadian Infantry Division's assault on Agira in late July 1943, Major-General Simonds' troops were forced to attack along the narrow Highway 121 corridor from Nissoria to Agira, so that their supporting armour could be utilised. In one engagement during the Canadians' struggle for Agira, the Royal Canadian Regiment lost fifty men while the Hastings and Prince Edward Island Regiment had another eighty casualties with no ground gained for their sacrifice. The British 231st Infantry, or Malta Brigade, incurred over 300 casualties, while all German losses numbered approximately 1,000. Shown above, a 25-pounder field-gun of the 7th Battery, 2nd Field Regiment, Royal Canadian Artillery fires on elements of the Italian Livorno and German 15th Panzergrenadier Divisions in the Nissoria-Agira corridor in late July. The final Canadian attack on Agira was supported by almost 100 25-pounder field-guns with this medieval central Sicilian town falling to them on 28 July. The British 25-pounder field-gun had been the standard field-gun for all Commonwealth forces with over 12,000 being produced from 1938 until the war's end. Its name came from the approximate weight of its ammunition and it was effective as a bombardment cannon as well as in an anti-tank role with its high-explosive and armour-piercing ammunition, respectively. *(NARA)*

(**Opposite page**) A Canadian infantryman with his No. 4 MkI(T) Short Magazine Lee-Enfield (SMLE) rifle with a sniper's No. 32 telescopic sight, detachable cheek rest, and a special leather sling was an effective combination to counter the ever-present German and Italian snipers, among other targets, as the Canadians advanced eastwards towards Adrano through both open country and central Sicilian towns. *(NARA)*

(**Above**) The undulating central Sicilian terrain comprised of rising hills and deep ravines near Caltanissetta where US II Corps infantry is shown marching in column. Caltanissetta was to the south-east of Enna, the latter of which the British 30th Corps had bypassed in Montgomery's mid-July change in strategic plan. After the invasion commenced, the Supreme Axis commander in Sicily, Italian General Alfredo Guzzoni, decided to move the 15th Panzergrenadier Division, which had just completed their move to western Sicily, returning it at once to resume a blocking position in the Caltanissetta area. Both the Americans and the Eighth Army's 30th Corps would have to contest this formidable German formation in the hilltop central Sicilian towns and villages as typified by terrain shown here. *(NARA)*

(**Opposite, above**) The combination of a poor road infrastructure within inland Sicily and congestion in offloading motor vehicles from the beachhead necessitated advancing units to be creative to hasten their deployment to targets removed from their landing areas. Here a column of American 82nd Airborne Division paratroopers are seen moving along a Sicilian dirt track in a procession of donkey carts that were ubiquitous on the island, as they were a major form of transportation for the local inhabitants. *(NARA)*

(**Opposite, below**) British Eighth Army soldiers of the Princess Patricia Canadian Light Infantry (PPCLI) move inland from their Pachino Peninsula landing areas towards Modica, to the south of Ragusa, on 12 July 1943, utilising local donkey carts to haul their heavier equipment along a lane lined with a wall separating it from an adjacent field. As is evident by the soldiers wearing shorts and open tunic blouses, the heat of an unshaded inland Sicilian coastal plain in July was oppressive to soldiers marching with full kit. As the Canadians had not campaigned with Montgomery's Desert Army in North Africa, many succumbed to heat and sun exposure-related maladies. Others, without adequately protecting their skin surface from mosquito bites, would contract malaria. *(NARA)*

## Chapter Three

# Commanders and Combatants

The Combined Chiefs of Staff again selected General Dwight D. Eisenhower to be the Supreme Commander for Operation *Husky*. Three of Britain's military leaders would comprise Eisenhower's land, sea and air commanders. General Harold Alexander would be Eisenhower's principal deputy and the Allied ground forces commander at his 15th Army Group headquarters. From there he would direct the US Seventh Army, under the command of Lieutenant-General George S. Patton, Jr., and the British Eighth Army, under General Bernard L. Montgomery. The senior Allied naval commander was the Royal Navy's Admiral Andrew Cunningham, who headed the Royal Navy's Mediterranean Fleet in 1943 and did not want to directly confront the Italian naval defences in the Messina and Augusta-Syracuse complexes. His US Navy counterpart was Vice Admiral H. Kent Hewitt, who had led the amphibious operations of the Western Task Force in the Moroccan invasion of November 1942. The senior Allied air commander was the Royal Air Force's Air Chief Marshal Arthur Tedder, who had commanded the Desert Air Force during the entire North African campaign.

The Allied invasion of Sicily was to utilise thirteen combat divisions and one independent brigade. In the Eighth Army sector, three divisions were to land along the Gulf of Noto on Sicily's eastern coast, while the 1st Canadian Infantry Division would land on the extreme south-eastern tip of the island. These troops were part of the Eastern Task Force (Force 545). British 13th Corps, under Lieutenant-General Miles Dempsey, would land as the Eighth Army's right with his British 5th Infantry Division (under Major-General H.P.M. Berney-Ficklin and after 3 August 1943 under Major-General G.C. Bucknall) landing near Cassibile and the 50th Infantry Division (under Major-General Sidney Kirkman) assaulting Avola; both locales were along Sicily's eastern coast in the Gulf of Noto. British Commando units were to land to the south of Syracuse and aid the British 5th Infantry Division to take the strategic port that Montgomery wanted to seize. British 30th Corps, under Lieutenant-General Oliver Leese, was to land his 51st Highland Division (under Major-General Douglas Wimberly) on the tip of the Pachino Peninsula. The 1st Canadian Infantry Division (under Major-General Guy G. Simonds) with two Royal Marine Commando units attached were to land on the western side of the Pachino Peninsula and capture the

Pachino airfield and make rendezvous with the Americans at Ragusa. The British Independent 231st Brigade, under the command of Brigadier Robert 'Roy' Urquhart, was to land to the north of Pachino in the Gulf of Noto. The British 1st Airlanding Brigade (under Brigadier P.H.W. 'Pip' Hicks) of the British 1st Airborne Division was to land via gliders, hours before the British and Canadian amphibious assaults, to capture the Ponte Grande Bridge over the Anapo River south of Syracuse, which commanded the approach to the port city of Syracuse. Other units of the British 1st Airborne Division (under Major-General George F. 'Hoppy' Hopkinson) were to be involved later in the campaign, notably in the parachute air-drop on Primosole Bridge on 13–14 July 1943.

For the amphibious invasion, the US Seventh Army, under the command of Patton (deputy commander Major-General Geoffrey Keyes), was comprised of the 2nd Armoured Division (under Major-General Hugh Gaffey), the 3rd Infantry Division (under Major-General Lucian Truscott), the 1st Infantry Division (under Major-General Terry de la Mesa Allen) and the 45th Infantry Division (under Major-General Troy Middleton). Comprising the assault troops of the Western Task Force (Force 343), the 1st, 3rd and 45th, were to assault beaches and seize airfields near the southern Sicilian towns of Gela, Licata and Scoglitti, respectively. Colonel James Gavin's 505th Parachute Infantry Regiment (PIR) of Major-General Matthew B. Ridgway's 82nd Airborne Division was reinforced with the 3rd Battalion, 504th PIR to form a regimental combat team of paratroopers to seize the Piano Lupo high ground inland from Gela several hours before the amphibious assault to disrupt any Axis counter-attack on the 1st Infantry Division beachhead. Piano Lupo referred to two hills that dominated a road junction where the Gela-Vittoria highway met a smaller road leading to Niscemi and the Ponte Olivo airfield. The US Army would also utilise its special forces of the 1st and 4th Ranger Battalions under the command of Lieutenant-Colonel William O. Darby (Darby's Force X), who had been leading these elite troops since their inception with Brigadier Truscott in Scotland in 1942.

From an operational standpoint, Lieutenant-General Omar Bradley would command US II Corps with a single corps headquarters comprising the 1st and 45th Infantry Divisions. Within days after the successful landings, and with Patton's movement to the west, a Provisional Corps Headquarters under Major-General Geoffrey Keyes would be established, to command a Provisional Corps made up of the 3rd Infantry, the 82nd Airborne and the 2nd Armoured Divisions, the latter of which was to follow the advance and exploit any breakthrough. Darby's Force X of the 1st and 4th Ranger Battalions would also be in the new Provisional Corps along with the 39th Infantry Regiment (led by Colonel H.A. 'Paddy' Flint) of the 9th Division (under Major-General Manton Eddy), which would reinforce these formations from North Africa after the landings.

On D-Day, the Allies would begin landing on Sicily with over 150,000 British, American, Canadian and French Moroccan troops, 14,000 vehicles, 600 tanks and 1,800 guns that were transported in a vast armada of over 2,500 ships of all types. In addition to the conventional assault forces of Eighth Army, the British would also employ elements of the 2nd Special Air Service, the British Commandos and Royal Marine Commandos. The mission of these elite British units was to seize targets in advance of the main assault and to destroy Axis coastal batteries.

Field Marshal Albert Kesselring, Senior Commander South, had the tactical authority over all German forces in Italy on the personal instruction of Adolf Hitler. His career was replete with tactical and organisational tasks, so he was well-suited for the role that he would play in repelling Operation *Husky*. Mussolini ordered General Alfredo Guzzoni out of retirement to take over the Sixth Army on Sicily in May 1943, which was, in effect, command of all armed forces on the island. Theoretically, Guzzoni held command over both Italian and German forces on Sicily. He replaced the former army commander, General Mario Roatta, who had tried to strengthen the defences on the island since February 1943. Guzzoni, like his predecessor, was also concerned about the inadequacies of air, naval and ground forces to defend the island.

Hitler ordered a corps commander headquarters positioned in southern Calabria to take over tactical command of all German forces if an invasion came. Its commander was General Hans Valentin Hube, a one-armed tank officer with a brilliant combat record on the Eastern Front. The Nazi führer also sent General Fridolin von Senger und Etterlin to Sicily as the *Wehrmacht* liaison officer to Guzzoni. Von Senger und Etterlin also shared Guzzoni's pessimism about the state of Sicily's defences against an Allied invasion.

To defend Sicily from an Allied invasion, the Axis fielded initially over 30,000 German ground troops and 240,000 Italian troops on the island with many other German formations proximate on the mainland. After the loss of Tunisia, Hitler, in response to an Italian request for *Wehrmacht* ground forces, sent elements of the newly-recreated Hermann Göring Division, the original one having been lost in northwest Africa. The Hermann Göring Division was to strengthen the recently-formed 15th Panzergrenadier Division, the latter of which was formed by amalgamating independent *Wehrmacht* units based on Sicily to the surviving veteran cadres of the battle-hardened 15th Panzer Division that had escaped from Tunisia. Just days prior to Operation *Husky*, both German divisions were in place to repel the Allied invasion. The Hermann Göring Division was commanded by paratrooper General Paul Conrath, who moved onto Sicily from southern Italy in June 1943. The 15th Panzergrenadier Division was commanded by General Eberhard Rodt. The Axis had approximately 260 tanks to defend Sicily with.

Hitler later sent two more elite divisions into Sicily to complement the Hermann Göring and 15th Panzergrenadier Divisions. These were the 29th Panzergrenadier and the elite *Luftwaffe* 1st Parachute Divisions, the latter with its four parachute regiments and ancillary artillery, AA, AT, signals and engineer units. The *Luftwaffe* 1st Parachute Division, under the command of Lieutenant-General Richard Heidrich, was formed in the early spring of 1943, mainly from the veteran German 7th Air Division. Issued with new weapons and trained intensively by Heidrich, the *Luftwaffe* 1st Parachute Division was regarded by the Allies as one of the very best German field forces. In July 1943, the total German strength on Sicily would number over 65,000 military personnel.

The Italian defenders on Sicily were comprised of two corps under Guzzoni's Sixth Army Command. These included six coastal divisions, two coastal brigades, one coastal regiment and four mobile divisions. The coastal divisions were relatively immobile and were of poor combat effectiveness as they lacked suitable weaponry and were also poorly led by their officers. The majority of troops in the coastal formations were Sicilian and their morale for continuing the war after an Allied invasion was low. The mobile Italian divisions were also comprised of native Sicilians and suffered similar shortcomings as their coastal counterparts. These included the Aosta, Napoli and Assietta Divisions. The fourth mobile Italian division, the Livorno Division, was somewhat more battle-worthy as it was at full strength with reasonable transport. Since the defenders anticipated an Allied move to quickly seize the Sicilian airfields, the Italians started work to surround the airfields with obstacles and fortified strongpoints comprised of concrete pillboxes and artillery pieces.

Major-General Geoffrey Keyes, the deputy commander of US Seventh Army (*left*); Brigadier-General Hobart Gay, Patton's Chief of Staff (*centre*); and Lieutenant-General George S. Patton, Jr., Commanding General US Seventh Army. They were aboard the USS *Monrovia* on 7 July 1943 *en route* to Sicily. Patton's previous command had been I Armoured Corps, as evidenced by the flag held by Keyes and worn by Patton as a shoulder patch. They all regard the new Seventh Army headquarters flag of Patton's new command. It was Vice-Admiral Hewitt who had presented Patton with his first Seventh Army flag. The unit bore the motto: 'Born at sea, Baptized in Blood.' Patton entered the Sicily campaign with only one corps headquarters, Bradley's US II Corps, since the headquarters of Patton's US I Armoured Corps had been augmented to create the new US Seventh Army counterpart. As this arrangement of only a single corps headquarters was proving impractical after the landings on Sicily, Patton added a Provisional Corps headquarters under his deputy, Keyes, to establish a more customary command hierarchy. Keyes, like Patton, was a West Point graduate, a veteran cavalryman, and was regarded as an intellectual soldier. After the 3rd Infantry Division captured Agrigento with Patton's famous reconnaissance in force, General Alexander, the 15th Army Group commander, approved continued American action in western Sicily. Keyes' Provisional Corps was comprised of the 3rd Infantry, 82nd Airborne, the 2nd Armoured (commanded by Major-General Hugh Gaffey) Divisions, along with Force X, consisting of two Ranger Battalions and the 39th Infantry Regiment of the 9th Division. This mobile formation was to begin its strike for Palermo on 19 July 1943, which fell to the Allies on 22 July. *(NARA)*

Lieutenant-General George S. Patton, Jr., commanding general of the US Seventh Army (*right*), Lieutenant-General Omar Bradley, commanding general of US II Corps, and Major-General Troy Middleton, commanding general of 45th Infantry Division, are seen going over plans in a Sicilian olive grove two weeks after the invasion started. Unlike Bradley and Patton, who were both graduates of West Point, Middleton enlisted in the army in 1910 and was commissioned a lieutenant before the First World War erupted. In 1918, Middleton was the youngest regimental commanding colonel in the American Expeditionary Force (AEF). Although he retired in 1937 to become the comptroller of Louisiana State University, he was recalled to active duty in 1941 after Pearl Harbor and then given command of the 45th Infantry Division, a National Guard unit from Oklahoma with a large percentage of its soldiers being Native American Indians. Countless books have been written about Patton and his military leadership. Suffice to say that for Operation *Husky*, he commanded the Seventh Army for the largest amphibious operation ever mounted at the time. Additionally, his westward thrust from the landing beaches to take Palermo and then place him to move on Messina along Sicily's northern coast contributed greatly to breaking the apparent stalemate affecting the British Eighth Army along Sicily's east coast narrow corridor dominated by Mount Etna. *(USAMHI)*

Major-General Lucian Truscott, Jr., commanding general of the 3rd Infantry Division, as shown here in North Africa wearing the distinctive shoulder patch of that illustrious unit. Truscott was a key officer, as a brigadier-general, in the development of the ranger battalions in the early days after American troops arrived in the United Kingdom. Then Truscott commanded the Sub-Task Force *Goalpost*, and was charged with the capture of the Mehdia-Port Lyautey area to secure the northern flank of the Western Task Force's assault on Morocco's Atlantic coast on 8 November 1942. After some hard fighting to achieve his objective, Eisenhower appointed the relatively junior Truscott to be his deputy Chief of Staff and representative for operations in Tunisia with his headquarters in Constantine. After the Vichy Armistice and amalgamation of French forces into the Allied Order of Battle, Eisenhower, through Truscott, would co-ordinate the parallel activities of the three national forces fighting the Axis in Tunisia. After the successful Tunisian campaign ended, Major-General Truscott would lead the 3rd Infantry Division in the invasion of Sicily, with the task of seizing the port of Licata and its airfield north-west of the city by the night of D-Day. After that, the 3rd Infantry Division, under Truscott, would spearhead Patton's advances to Agrigento, Palermo and then, along the northern coast to Messina. *(NARA)*

(**Opposite, above**) Major-General Manton S. Eddy (*left*), commanding general of the US 9th Infantry Division in Bizerte, with his Assistant Division commander, Brigadier-General Daniel Stroh (*right*), are shown after the capture of that Tunisian city from the Axis defenders on 8 May 1943. The 9th Infantry Division would serve as Patton's Seventh Army's reserve, with its 39th Infantry Regiment and accompanying artillery ready to move to Sicily when needed after 10 July 1943. Once Palermo was captured on 22 July, the first convoys into the capital city's harbour transported the remaining units from Eddy's 9th Infantry Division. After the exhausted US 1st Infantry Division took Troina, it was Eddy's 9th Infantry Division that provided their long-overdue relief. After the 9th Infantry Division took part in the closing chapter of the Sicily campaign, Eddy led his unit into Normandy in 1944. In August 1944, Patton had him lead US Third Army's XII Corps, which spearheaded the advance across France and then into Germany. *(NARA)*

(**Opposite, below**) Major-General Terry de la Mesa Allen (*left*), commanding general of the US 1st Infantry Division (the 'Big Red One'), with his superior, Lieutenant-General Omar Bradley, commander of US II Corps, which did the bulk of the fighting in central Sicily after advancing from the Gela and Scoglitti beachheads. Here the two generals are shown going over maps for the assault on Troina in central Sicily. The relief of both Allen and his assistant division commander, Brigadier-General Theodore Roosevelt, Jr., temporally coincident with the climax of the fighting for Troina and had caused controversy. According to official records, although Patton had personally requested Allen lead his 1st Infantry Division into combat for Operation *Husky*, he also wanted to replace him with Major-General Clarence R. Huebner 'without prejudice' and mainly 'due to nothing else but weariness, occasioned by long and intensive efforts on the battlefields'. Patton wanted Allen to be given a command back in the United States since he had been involved in the fighting since Operation *Torch* on 8 November 1942. Unfortunately, the orders for the change of command of the 1st Infantry Division arrived at the peak of the brutal combat for Troina rather than after its successful completion. Although records claim that Patton insisted Allen stay on until 'you've taken Troina and the 1st Division has completed its job in Sicily', the reason for his relief and by whom was controversial. Nonetheless, Allen took over the command of the 104th Infantry Division, which saw action in north-west Europe. *(Author's Collection)*

BRADLEY

Major-General Matthew B. Ridgway, commanding general of the 82nd Airborne Division, is shown reviewing plans with some of this staff officers at Ribera on Sicily after the invasion. The 82nd Airborne division had a stellar history having fought in a regular infantry capacity in the First World War in the Meuse-Argonne and St Mihiel battles of the American Expeditionary Force (AEF). The infantry division was reactivated in 1942, when it was commanded by Major-General Omar Bradley. It was selected to become the first of the new airborne divisions and Ridgway was given command of it in its new mission. Ridgway was a West Point graduate who was committed to not squandering his troops and always respected the ordinary soldiers. The decision for the elements of the 82nd Airborne to jump into Sicily at night to avoid enemy fighters and anti-aircraft (AA) guns during daylight, coupled with strong winds and inexperienced aircrews, contributed to the scattering of these paratrooper forces on D-Day. *(NARA)*

Brigadier Theodore Roosevelt, Jr. is shown sitting on his Jeep 'Rough Rider'. He was the eldest son of the former president and commanded one of the 1st Infantry Division's battalions in France in 1918 and was both wounded and gassed during combat. After serving as the governor of Puerto Rico and governor-general of the Philippines, Roosevelt returned to active service in early 1941 to command his old regiment, the 26th Infantry, as a colonel. Upon being promoted to brigadier-general, he became General Allen's assistant division commander in the 'Big Red One'. He had a reputation for fearlessness in combat and exuded devotion to his infantrymen, even though his military appearance was sometimes referred to as 'dishevelled'. After his relief with Allen after Troina, Roosevelt would go on to be first a liaison officer in Italy and then the assistant division commander for the 4th Infantry Division. In that latter capacity, he would provide invaluable leadership at Utah Beach in Normandy on another D-Day, 6 June 1944, for which he won the Congressional Medal of Honour. *(NARA)*

Major-General Guy G. Simonds, commander of the 1st Canadian Infantry Division, is shown coming ashore wearing both binoculars and an inflatable life vest at the *Bark West* beachhead near Pachino on Sicily's south-eastern tip. By the end of the Sicily campaign, Simonds and his Canadian soldiers were very well respected by Montgomery. Later in north-west Europe as a corps commander, Simonds would remain highly regarded as a strong combat leader. *(NARA)*.

(**Opposite, above**) Lieutenant-General Miles Dempsey, the commanding general of British 13th Corps, is shown meeting with British Eighth Army commander Bernard L. Montgomery as they review operational plans and maps on the bonnet of a car. Dempsey landed in the Gulf of Noto commanding the British 5th Infantry and 50th Northumbrian Divisions. Once Montgomery was assured of the success of Eighth Army's landings, Dempsey was told to move quickly on Syracuse and then Augusta on Sicily's eastern coast. Syracuse had indeed fallen to 13th Corps quickly by 11 July, with its port facilities undamaged. Dempsey's corps was preparing for a major thrust into the Plain of Catania on the night of 13 July. However, a German paratrooper regiment was air-dropped and along with additional *Wehrmacht* infantry battalions and a subsequent concentration of enemy forces would severely retard the movement of Dempsey's corps towards both Catania and the ultimate strategic goal, Messina. As with Patton, numerous tomes have already been written about Montgomery. Suffice to say that in regards to Operation *Husky*, Montgomery in the spring of 1943 was appalled by the lack of direction for the upcoming operation and an Allied 'planning rift' ensued with much debate about the strategy and tactics to seize Sicily. On 2 May, in the Allied Forces Headquarters (AFHQ) lavatory, Montgomery explained his plan to Eisenhower's Chief of Staff, Major-General Walter Bedell Smith, to cancel a separate American landing at Palermo and instead shifted Patton's Seventh Army effort to the Licata-Gela-Scoglitti area along Sicily's south-eastern coast to capture the Axis airfields and serve as a left flank for the British Eighth Army landing in the Gulf of Noto and on the south-eastern tip near Pachino. *(Author's Collection)*

(**Opposite, below**) British 30th Corps commander, Lieutenant-General Oliver Leese (*second from left*), is shown addressing some Canadian officers, including the 1st Canadian Infantry Division commander, Major-General Guy G. Simonds (*far left*). Leese was commissioned in the Coldstream Guards and served during the First World War, winning medals, but also suffering three wounds. During the Second Battle of El Alamein and the pursuit of Rommel, Leese commanded 30th Corps and was able to get the best out of his divisional commanders, such as the New Zealander, Bernard Freyberg. *(NARA)*

Major-General Vyvyan Evelegh (*second from right*), General Officer Commanding (GOC) the British 78th Infantry Division, is shown reviewing some map co-ordinates with Brigadier E.E.E. Cass of the British 11th Brigade (*far right*), and American colonels George A. Smith, Jr. and Harry A. 'Paddy' Flint of the US 18th (1st Division) and 39th (9th Division) Infantry Regiments, respectively. The quartet of Allied officers met at Randazzo as the Eighth and Seventh Armies converged on Messina. The 39th Infantry Regiment had arrived on Sicily on 15 July, and was with Keyes' Provisional Corps in western Sicily and the assault on Palermo. The 39th Infantry Regiment, along with Moroccan Goums, had been hastily transferred to the II Corps area of Bradley's operations in central Sicily and had been attached to the 1st Infantry Division for the Troina battle. Colonel 'Paddy' Flint was one of Patton's oldest friends and, as such, had been placed in charge of the 39th Infantry Regiment to give it some fighting spirit. He died of a sniper's bullet as he led his troops with his customary *élan*, attacking an enemy position in Normandy on 24 July 1944. Colonel Smith commanded the 18th Infantry Regiment through to the end of February 1945. (*USAMHI*)

(**Left**) Field Marshal Albert Kesselring, a *Luftwaffe* officer, was appointed Commander-in-Chief South in December 1941 with his headquarters based near Rome. Prior to that, Kesselring helped create the operational mechanics of the *Luftwaffe*, commanded Hitler's air squadrons in the Mediterranean theatre, and reported to the Italian fascist leader, Benito Mussolini, as well. Having combat experience in both Poland and France, he was instrumental in the development of tactical aerial assault, notably with his squadrons of Ju 87 or *Stuka* dive bombers in 1939 and 1940, which he brought to the Mediterranean theatre along the North African littoral. During the Sicily campaign, Kesselring retained tactical authority over all German military units in Italy, even though he was a *Luftwaffe* rather than an army officer. *(NARA)*

(**Centre**) Recalled out of retirement since May 1941, Italian General Alfredo Guzzoni, commander of the Italian Sixth Army, who was given responsibility for Sicily's defence by the Axis forces in late May 1943 against an anticipated Allied invasion, is shown. He and Kesselring shared fundamental differences as to how best to protect Sicily's 600 miles of coastline in the event of an amphibious assault. Guzzoni had been the commander of the Italian Expeditionary force in Albania and then in Greece, where setbacks in the latter country resulted in his recall to Italy. On inspection of the defences of Sicily, Guzzoni found that the ground, air and naval forces were not up to the task of repelling an invasion, despite adequate troop numbers. What appalled him was the dismal morale and lack of training. Guzzoni did not fall for Allied deception plots and correctly believed that the Allied invasion would come to Sicily's south-eastern sector. Rather than defend the entire Sicilian coastline, Guzzoni's preference was to mass a powerful counter-attack at the landing beaches, utilising German Panzer formations on the island as his instrument. Kesselring disagreed with this tactic and, although he too believed the south-eastern sector to be the likely target, he dispersed his armour by placing the German 15th Panzergrenadier Division in western Sicily. *(NARA)*

(**Right**) German General Hans Valentin Hube, commanding general of the *Wehrmacht's* XIVth Panzer Corps stationed in Reggio di Calabria across the Strait of Messina from Sicily. Hube was a Panzer army commander on the Russian front and despite having lost an arm in the First World War was considered to be one of the most able of the German armoured commanders. In addition to dispatching the *Luftwaffe's* 1st Parachute Division to the island, Kesselring ordered Hube, with Hitler's approval, to move the 29th Panzergrenadier Division from Calabria to Sicily on 18 July 1943 in order to defend a stout line in front of Mount Etna. *(NARA)*

(**Left**) German General Paul Conrath, who commanded the Hermann Göring Division, a *Luftwaffe* Panzergrenadier formation, is shown. Much of the original division had been sent to the Tunisian bridgehead to aid von Arnim. However, it was ultimately lost in May 1943. The Germans in this division had been some of the last to surrender from their cave redoubts to the Allies on 10 May. A reconstituted division of *Luftwaffe* personnel began arriving in Sicily in mid-June 1943. Conrath was aggressive and experienced as well as enjoying Göring's favour, even though he was given only two of the four Panzergrenadier regiments that had been stationed in France and then southern Italy. However, Conrath was given a company of Mk VI 'Tiger' tanks that had been appropriated from the 15th Panzergrenadier Division. Just prior to the invasion, the arrival of the Hermann Göring Division in Sicily had been accomplished. The majority of Conrath's forces were located in south-eastern Sicily, while roughly a third was situated in the vicinity of Catania on the eastern coast. Conrath's divisional headquarters was 20 miles north-east of Gela, at Caltagirone, from where he would direct repeated German armoured counter-attacks against the US 1st Infantry Division bridgehead on 10 and 11 July 1943. *(NARA)*

(**Centre**) General Fridolin von Senger und Etterlin was one of many well-educated Prussian aristocratic officers who had decided to fight for their country even though their religious and political views were at odds with Hitler's brutal Nazi regime. A First World War veteran field artilleryman and a post-war Weimar cavalryman, this staunch Catholic was tasked for the upcoming Sicily invasion with a vague role as the German liaison officer to the Italian Sixth Army on the island and to save the Nazi forces should the Italians become treacherous and seek a separate surrender. Von Senger had been a brigade commander during the *blitzkrieg* in France in the spring of 1940 and led the 17th Panzer Division during the winter campaign of 1942 on the Russian Front. Upon arriving on Sicily in late June 1943, Senger und Etterlin was shocked by the incomplete and disorganised Italian defences of the island's coastline. Furthermore, he became aware that most of the German air assets had been sent to Sardinia in the event of an invasion there. *(NARA)*

(**Right**) German General Eberhard Rodt, commander of the newly formed 15th Panzergrenadier Division. This battle-ready division was already stationed on Sicily before the invasion in July 1943. It was named for the 15th Panzer Division, which was lost during the Axis surrender of their Tunisian bridgehead during the first week of May 1943. Utilizing a variety of German units present in Sicily, this division was reconstituted initially under the command of Colonel Ernst-Guenther Baade, until Rodt took over from him on 5 June 1943. *(NARA)*

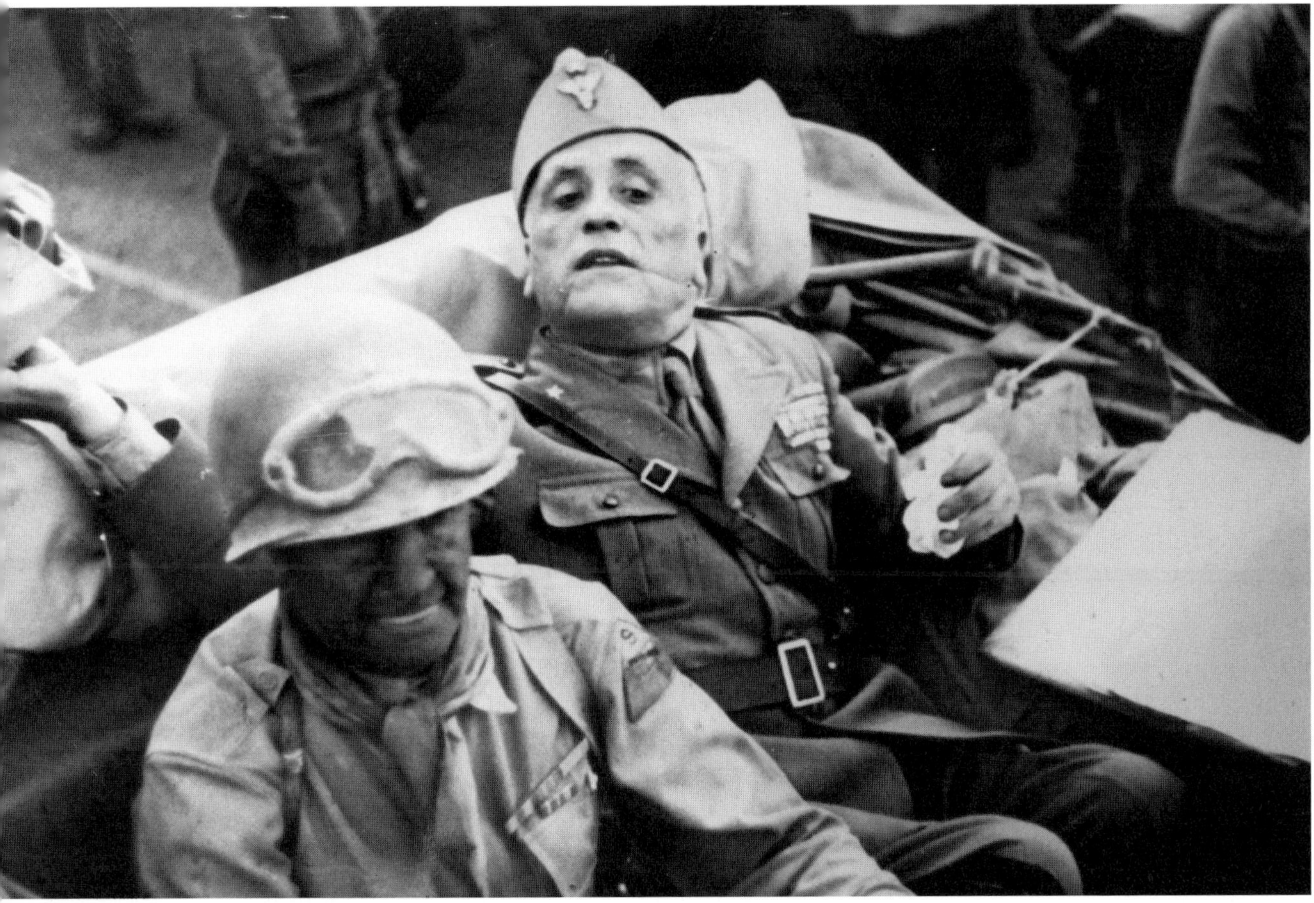

Major-General Geoffrey Keyes, Patton's US Seventh Army deputy and Provisional Corps commander (*left*) with the captured, scar-faced Italian General Giuseppe Molinero, commander of Port Defence North, are shown after the surrender of Palermo to the Allies. Patton had unleashed his mobile Provisional Corps, under Keyes, from 19–22 July 1943, which caused the war-weary Italian port defences commander to surrender rather than fight a protracted urban battle once the Germans had left the capital city of 400,000 inhabitants. Molinero was taken to Keyes and Major-General Hugh Gaffey, the 2nd Armoured Corps commander. Then Keyes and Molinero rode in a procession to Palermo's Royal Palace to accept the Italian surrender of the city at 1900hrs on 22 July. *(USAMHI)*

American Lieutenant-Colonel H.C. Lyons of the Seventh Army conversing with Italian General Giovanni Marciani, commander of the 206th Coastal Division, in Palermo, as negotiations to surrender the city to Patton's forces were underway. By the evening of 22 July 1943, two American divisions, the 3rd Infantry and 2nd Armoured, entered the city after the Germans had already evacuated Palermo and the Italian military leaders defending it no longer wanted to fight. *(NARA)*

Colonel James M. Gavin, a West Point graduate commander of the 82nd Airborne Division's 505th Parachute Infantry Regiment (PIR), is seen talking with a bearded *Chicago Tribune* war correspondent John H. 'Beaver' Thompson, a veteran of North Africa jumps, at Biazza Ridge on Sicily on 11 July 1943. It was at this site near the Gela invasion beach that Gavin and his paratroopers resisted a German counter-attack. The 82nd Airborne Division's commanding general, Major-General Matthew B. Ridgway, later said of his 505th PIR commander that he 'developed into one of the finest battle leaders, and one of the most brilliant thinkers, the Army has produced'. *(NARA)*

(**Opposite, above**) Members of the 3rd Battalion of the 504th Parachute Infantry Regiment (PIR) are seen checking their parachute harnesses and equipment as they prepare to board their C-47 'Skytrain' transport for their air-drop onto Sicily on 9–10 July 1943. Over 250 C-47 aircraft of the 52nd Troop Carrier Wing of the US Army Air Force (USAAF) moved the more than 3,400 paratroopers of Colonel Gavin's Combat Team 505, comprising the 505th PIR, reinforced with the 3rd Battalion of the 504th PIR, from Tunisian bases to over Sicily to operationally land in four drop-zones to Gela's north-east during Operation *Husky* 1, the preliminary American airborne assault. These paratroopers were to seize the high ground, Piano Lupo, in the Gela area and prevent the enemy from counter-attacking the enemy beachhead later on D-Day. *(NARA)*

(**Opposite, below**) Lieutenant-Colonel Charles W. Kouns is shown giving members of his parachute battalion some last minute instruction aboard their C-47 'Skytrain' transport over the Mediterranean *en route* to Sicily. He exhorted them, 'Your destination is the Italian island of Sicily and you will be the first American troops to land'. *(NARA)*

D-1
11834

Lieutenant-Colonel (shown here in Scotland as a major) William O. Darby, commander of the 1st and 4th Ranger Battalions of Force X ('Darby's Rangers'). Darby was a West Point graduate who initially started soldiering as an officer in the army's last horse artillery unit. He gained notoriety as a trainer of a specialised US Army unit that was to be modelled on the British Commandos. Brigadier-General Truscott, who oversaw the unit's training first in Northern Ireland and then in Scotland before the North African invasion said of Darby, 'Never in this war have I known a more gallant, heroic officer.' In fact, it was Truscott who selected the name 'Rangers' for this unit based on the pre-Revolutionary War colonial unit that went by the same name after being formed by Major Robert Rogers to fight alongside the British during the French and Indian War. Darby would be awarded a Distinguished Service Cross (DSC) for his action in procuring a 37mm anti-tank (AT) gun and destroying an Italian tank with it in Gela on 10 July 1943. *(USAMHI)*

(**Opposite, above**) Some of the rangers from Darby's 1st Battalion are seen relaxing while another is vigilant manning his 0.30in-calibre Browning light machine-gun at a captured French fort at Arzew near Oran on 8 November 1942, the D-Day for Operation *Torch* and the Allied invasion of north-west Africa. The invasion planners for *Torch* knew that the Rangers and the US 1st Infantry Division might be engaged by Vichy's Oran Division of 10,000 men. The 'Big Red One' and the Ranger Battalion, having demonstrated a strong combat *élan* with its capable commanders at Oran, convinced Patton that these units had to land at Gela, which the *Husky* planners envisioned would be the toughest American assault zone. *(NARA)*

(**Opposite, below**) Members of the British 1st Airborne Division's 1st Airlanding Brigade, comprised of 2,100 glidermen commanded by Brigadier Philip H.W. 'Pip' Hicks, was to arrive near Syracuse on 9–10 July 1943 and be the spearhead of the British Eighth Army. In this photograph they are shown checking their equipment before boarding their gliders near Kaiouran airfield in Tunisia before the Allied airborne operations of Operation *Husky* began on 9 July. Their mission, Operation *Ladbroke*, was to seize and hold the bridge over the Anapo River, the Ponte Grande, until relieved by elements of the British 5th Division, commanded by Major-General H.P.M. Berney-Ficklin. The major obstacle to the capture of Syracuse was the Ponte Grande Bridge and Montgomery's selection of this elite unit was to prevent enemy control of it to allow for British vehicular traffic to move rapidly on toward Syracuse. The 1st Airlanding Brigade consisted of: the 1st Battalion, The Border Regiment; the 2nd Battalion, The South Staffordshire Regiment; and the 9th Field Company, Royal Engineers. The brigade was to go into Sicily with only six Jeep-towed 6-pounder anti-tank (AT) guns and ten 3in mortars, in addition to individual weapons carried by each gliderman. The British glidermen were in mostly Waco C-4A or 'Hadrian' glider aircraft, since there were only a handful of the larger British 'Horsa' gliders available in the theatre. *(Author's Collection)*

British glider pilots are shown being briefed in early July for airborne assault, Operation *Ladbroke*. These men were all volunteers of the Glider Pilot Regiment formed in 1942 to carry the Airborne's glidermen into combat. Once firmly on the ground, the glider pilots had been trained to operate any infantry weapon, radio or vehicle, and, in essence, function as airborne infantrymen to seize the objective usually in a *coup de main* style. A British paratrooper officer quipped, 'I thanked God that I went to battle by parachute and not by glider.' Other paratroopers referred to the gliders as 'flying coffins'. *(Author's Collection)*

A C-47 'Skytrain' cargo plane, which the British referred to as the 'Dakota', is seen practising take-off and towing of a Waco CG-4A glider from an airfield in North Africa in June 1943, just weeks before the airborne parachute drops. This extremely versatile aircraft was modified for military use from the civilian Douglas DC-3 twin-engine airliner. The C-47 was used in all Allied theatres of operation in the Second World War for both troop-carrying and re-supply missions, and, where feasible, medical evacuation. Although thoroughly trained, the 82nd Airborne Division's glidermen were disgruntled as they would not participate in the American airborne operations of 9–10 July. The British Waco CG-4A or 'Hadrian' gliders were towed by C-47 'Dakotas' as well as Halifax and Albemarle medium bombers, which were needed to tow the larger but fewer 'Horsa' gliders utilised in the airborne operations. *(USAMHI)*

A Moroccan Goum is shown sharpening his bayonet for his rifle slung across his back. He wore the classic woollen, striped *djellbah* of the mountain tribesmen, who were known for their ferocity against Axis soldiers, especially with their knives and bayonets. *(USAMHI)*

(**Above**) A Royal Australian Air Force (RAAF) airman is seen scanning the sky with his binoculars as he manned his Bofors anti-aircraft (AA) artillery piece on a rooftop in Pachino. The RAAF had a contingent of P-40 'Kittyhawk' planes and aircrews on Sicily to provide fighter-bomber tactical support. *(AWM)*

(**Opposite page**) British Royal Air Force (RAF) Servicing Commandos took cover along the side of a bomb crater at a recently-captured airfield in the Gerbini complex in the Plain of Catania as a German bomber passed overhead. *(NARA)*

(**Opposite page**) US Navy Lieutenant Livingston Harley loaded leaflets into a 105mm shell to be fired into Axis positions encouraging the enemy to surrender rather than continue fighting. Many Italian soldiers readily capitulated to Allied troops. However, German units, especially the paratroopers fighting as infantry, were tenacious in holding onto their defensive works as long as possible before withdrawing, usually after sowing mines and demolishing roadways and bridges. *(NARA)*

(**Above**) American field artilleryman Harold Bergman is shown with his field piece in Sicily. Stencilled onto the shield of his gun are the Tunisian battles that he and his crew fought in during the North African campaign before Operation *Husky*. Unlike the majority of British Eighth Army troops and commanders, the landings in Morocco and Algeria and the subsequent six-month Tunisian campaign was the Americans' 'baptism of fire' in the European theatre. *(NARA)*

Two Canadian officers of the 48th Highlanders of Canada are shown wearing the traditional Scottish Glengarry creased woollen cap with short ribbons on the back (*left*) and Tam-o'-shanter woollen hat with a pom-pom in the centre of it (*right*). They are seen reviewing maps laid out on the back of a scout car in a Sicilian fruit orchard. (*NARA*)

A Canadian tanker of the Canadian 1st Army Tank Brigade, wearing his black beret, is shown setting up communications with his field telephone on the steps of a building in a south-eastern Sicilian town. (*NARA*)

An American captain is shown inspecting a German 21cm rocket gun or *Nebelwerfer* ('Smoke Launcher') on Sicily. During the war, the *Wehrmacht* used a large number of artillery weapons firing rocket-propelled ammunition with the *Nebelwerfer* being the best known. This 21cm *Nebelwerfer* 42 could launch rocket-propelled projectiles from all of its five tubes within eight seconds. (*NARA*)

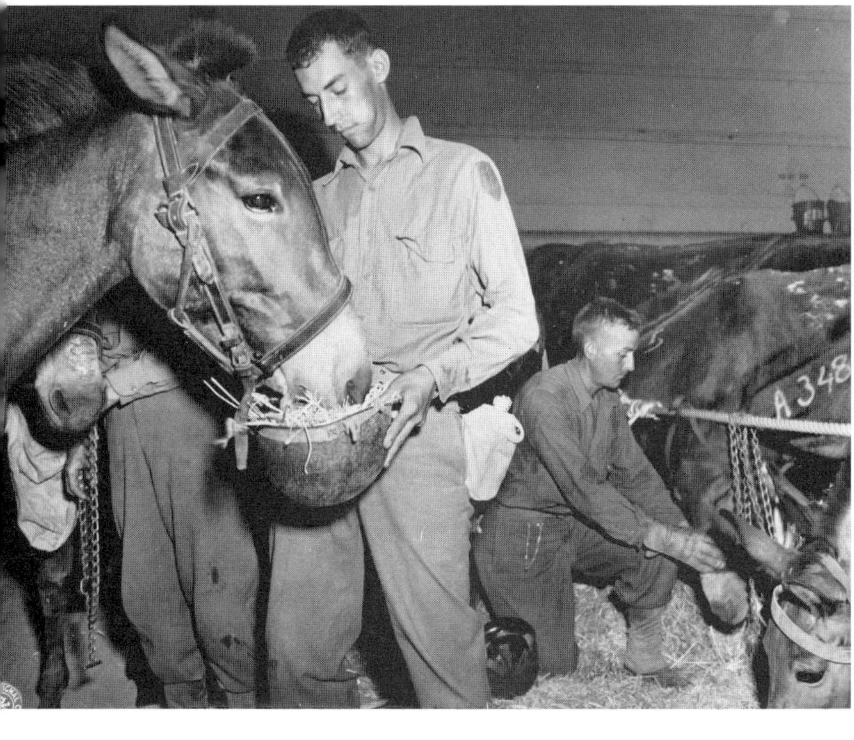

An American mule-handler is seen feeding his charge hay from a helmet. These invaluable mules were aboard ship for transport to Palermo towards the end of July to participate in the US Seventh Army's Provisional Corps eastward advance along the mountainous northern coast of Sicily towards Messina. These sure-footed animals could carry an incredible pack weight providing all essentials to troops on the front-lines. (*NARA*)

(**Opposite, above**) American Lieutenant John Armolino is shown manning his Jeep's monopod-mounted machine-gun as the vehicle and crew edge slowly backwards towards Troina in the closing days of the 1st Infantry Division assault on the central Sicilian mountaintop town. The backward movement would enable the Jeep to rapidly escape if they came under concealed enemy fire. Another Jeep with its 0.50in-calibre machine-gun pointed skywards is in the background on the road as a plane flies off above the mountains in the distance. *(NARA)*

(**Opposite, below**) Two British Eighth Army tankers are seen examining a 2-man 'Italian' tank near Rosolini, 25 miles to the south-west of Syracuse on Sicily's eastern coast. By the tank's profile appearance, this was probably a commandeered Renault R-35 Light tank that made it into the Italian armoured formations after the French capitulation of June 1940. The main 37mm gun was unable to penetrate even light German armour in 1940, thus it was no match for the heavier Allied tanks of 1943, principally the M4 'Sherman'. *(NARA)*

(**Above**) American engineers of the 1st Battalion of the 39th Combat Engineers in Gela with their 'bazookas' after a failed Italian motorised counter-attack on the port city on 10 July 1943. The term 'bazooka' appears to have been derived from a radio musician/comic who used a similar looking instrument in his act. The engineers assisted Colonel Darby's Force X, comprised of the 1st and 4th Ranger Battalions. The engineers used their bazookas in a formidable fashion against the lightly armoured Italian tanks. The M1 bazooka made its combat debut as a high-performance, infantry-based anti-tank (AT) weapon against the German Panzers in Tunisia. In 1943, an improved M1A1 model, with an improved aiming system, was utilised. After its development, an individual infantryman could combat heavily armoured targets at over 200yds distance. Also, there was no recoil as the propulsive jet from the rocket exited rearward out of the open barrel. *(NARA)*

British mortar men loading a 20lb bomb into the tube of their new M2 4.2in mortar, which fired the round 4,000yds on the Adrano Front. This mortar was an improvement over the M1 Chemical Mortar, which entered service in 1928, with the M2 entering service in early 1943. Its 4ft tube, which weighed 105lb, was rifled and the weapon had a range of 560 to 4,400yds. It was very suitable for Sicily since this weapon could be utilised in rough terrain, such as mountains. There, rounds would have to be fired onto enemy positions along reverse slopes with 'plunging' bombardment rather than direct fire. Also, it was extremely difficult to transport artillery pieces into those locales. *(NARA)*

Two British infantrymen lying near a culvert as they prepare to fire the Projector Infantry Anti-Tank (PIAT) Mk 1. This new infantry anti-tank (AT) weapon made its combat debut during the Sicily invasion. It was designed in 1942 when the British needed an effective, inexpensive portable AT weapon for infantrymen. The weapon's design was based on the spigot mortar system that launched a 2.5lb bomb using a spring and a cartridge in the tail of the projectile. The weight of the PIAT was 32lb unloaded and had an operational range of 115yds for direct fire against armoured vehicles, and 350yds in an indirect fire mode against bunkers or fortified houses. There was no muzzle smoke to give away the location of the crew. However, there was a powerful recoil and some difficulty in cocking the spring mechanism. *(USAMHI)*

A battery of four British 25-pounder field cannons firing on the Axis escape route from Messina from the vicinity of Mount Etna near Zafferana Etnea, located 12 miles north of Catania. From 1938 onwards, the 25-pounder was the standard field cannon of all Commonwealth forces playing a major role in the desert campaign before adequate anti-tank (AT) guns, such as the 6-pounder, arrived. It was called the 25-pounder because of the approximate weight of the ammunition (both high explosive and armour-piercing). The mount of the gun allowed it to be aimed high, like a Howitzer, but it had a circular disk that could be lowered to the ground so the gunners could turn the weapon 360 degrees quickly for AT combat. *(NARA)*

A British 'Bishop' self-propelled artillery (SPA) vehicle of the type that saw action with the 142nd Field Regiment in Sicily in late July 1943 is shown in profile. The 'Bishop' had a crew of four for its armour-protected 25-pounder mounted field-gun. The 'Bishop' first appeared in service in North Africa to give the 25-pounder crews some armoured protection from high explosive (HE) enemy shells and continued to see action on Sicily and the Italian mainland. Its major deficiencies were its slow maximal road speed of 15mph, a limited gun elevation and traverse as well as a congested crew space. The 'Bishop' had its 25-pounder mounted on a Valentine tank chassis, which gave it both fording and vertical obstacle-clearing of about 3ft. The British also removed the turret from the Canadian-produced Ram tank (replaced by the American M3), and after mounting the standard British 25-pounder gun, the 'Sexton', another SPA vehicle was created, which saw action in north-west Europe in 1944 and 1945. *(USAMHI)*

A shirtless British Royal Artillery crew wearing khaki shorts in the intense heat fire their 5.5in Mk 2 field cannon at Axis forces reeling back towards their escape route at Messina. This artillery piece was first introduced in the army in May 1942, and it was deployed in the North African campaign. With a new 20lb lighter high explosive (HE) shell, the maximum range of the gun improved considerably to just over 9 miles. *(NARA)*

A British Universal Carrier is shown travelling across Primosole Bridge, which spanned the Simeto River a few miles south of Catania, after the battle was over. On the night of 13 July, the British 1st Parachute Brigade, under the command of Brigadier C.W. Lathbury, received orders confirming they would depart from their Tunisian airfields in C-47 'Dakota' and Albemarle medium bombers to air-drop around and attack the Primosole Bridge that night to secure the line of advance to Catania. The 'Red Devils' were to be preceded by an air-drop of the Pathfinders from the 21st Independent Company. The British 1st Parachute Brigade had 1,900 of its men take off from North Africa, but only about 250 men from the 1st and 3rd Battalions were successfully air-dropped. Three hours later, eleven Horsa gliders were to land in the vicinity of the bridge-carrying AT guns, gunners, sappers and field ambulances. During the early morning hours of 14 July, a contingent of fifty British paratroopers reached the bridge and seized it from Italian troops, who had fled in panic when one of the British gliders crashed into the bridge. A group of *Fallschirmjägers* from the 4th German Parachute Regiment, reinforced by some German tanks from Catania, attacked the weakly held British positions on the bridge and evicted the British paratroopers, numbering only just over 100, after the 'Red Devils' had kept the bridge in their possession for sixteen hours. Lathbury withdrew his small paratrooper contingent from Primosole Bridge to a small perimeter south of the bridge, where the 'Red Devils' held out waiting for relief. Within a few hours of ceding the bridge to the Germans, British paratroopers of the 2nd Battalion (commanded by Lieutenant-Colonel John Frost), who had been in action in the hills south of the river and borne the brunt of the German counter-attacks during the first hours of daylight on 14 July, were relieved by tanks of the 4th Armoured Brigade, which arrived from the invasion beaches, accompanied by soldiers of the British Durham Light Infantry (DLI) Regiment, who had made a forced march of 25 miles. The British troops, reinforcing the 'Red Devils' continued to attack the German paratrooper positions and after two days of ferocious battle and heavy casualties, they found that on 16 July the German bridge defenders had gone after holding back the British advance. *(Author's Collection)*

(**Above**) Members of a German paratrooper anti-tank (AT) unit are seen manning their Pak 38 50mm weapon in the Primosole Bridge vicinity in mid-July 1943. Because the Pak 38 was very heavy, it was usually towed into position by a tractor. It had an effective range of approximately 1.5 miles. Earlier, on 13 July, the German 1st Parachute Division, under General Richard Heidrich, had flown from Rome and parachuted or air-landed in the Catania area. *(Author's Collection)*

(**Opposite, above**) German paratroopers of the 1st Parachute Machine-Gun Battalion, which had air-landed at Catania on 13 July 1943, are shown manning their Universal Machine-Gun (MG) Model 42 to lay withering fire on 14 July, to beat back a British attack by troops of the Durham Light Infantry (DLI) in the vicinity of Primosole Bridge. This belt-fed MG had a firing rate of 1,500 rounds per minute. It was one of, if not the best, MGs of the Second World War. Unlike its predecessor, the MG 34, it was not prone to malfunction with rough elements such as mud and snow. *(Author's Collection)*

(**Opposite, below**) This German soldier was killed in combat south of Enna by Canadians of the Carleton and York Regiment. The Axis defences in the vicinity of Enna had been manned by elements of the German 15th Panzer-grenadier Division along with Italians of the Livorno Division. *(NARA)*

A dead German tanker is sprawled in the left foreground after having been blasted from his Mk IV Panzer, which is inspected by a US 3rd Division infantryman at Cape Orlando, to the west of Brolo, on Sicily's northern coast. The tank was destroyed by direct fire from an American anti-tank (AT) gun. *(NARA)*

A German motorcyclist's corpse is seen lying dead next to his vehicle after he was killed by paratroopers of the American 505th Parachute Infantry Regiment (PIR) to the north of Gela on 10 July 1943. The 505th PIR was tasked to interdict any Axis counter-attack on the Gela beachhead, which the US 1st Infantry Division along with Ranger battalions was attempting to consolidate. *(NARA)*

Three German airmen are photographed sitting in a composed manner after they were captured at an airfield in south-eastern Sicily very early after the invasion started. They sit on the beach under British guard awaiting transport back to stockades in North Africa. *(NARA)*

(**Opposite, above**) A group of Germans captured in western Sicily by elements of the 3rd US Infantry Division are herded together for a march back to the rear and imprisonment. Although they appear bewildered and 'shell-shocked', these German troops put up a tenacious defence, unlike some of the Italian coastal units, which readily surrendered to the advancing Americans of the Provisional Corps under Major-General Keyes. *(USAMHI)*

(**Opposite, below**) The crew of an Italian field Howitzer is shown manning their rapid-fire gun for action. The Italian Sixth Army on Sicily, although it had been based there since the autumn of 1941, was not adequately prepared for the invasion since its defences had been hardly strengthened during the nearly two year interval. Also, the staggering losses incurred by Italian formations in the Western Desert, Ethiopia, north-west Africa, and the Russian Front depleted the Sicilian formations of adequate transport, armour and leadership. Nonetheless, the artillery remained a potent and respected arm of Mussolini's army despite their antiquated ordnance. *(NARA)*

(**Above**) A dead Italian gunner is shown near his small calibre anti-tank (AT) gun. The gallantry of the Italian artilleryman, in contrast to the problematic reputation of the fighting spirit of the infantry, was often ignored as many of the gunners fought valiantly and died around their own antiquated field weapons. Among the Sicilian coastal divisions, Italian infantrymen and artillerymen used captured pieces from previously- vanquished Axis opponents, such as the French, Czechs and Greeks. *(NARA)*

Part of a British infantry section is seen passing the corpses of dead Italian soldiers in Avola, located along the Gulf of Noto midway between Pachino to the south and Syracuse to the north. On D-Day, a group of seventy-five American paratroopers of the 505th Parachute Infantry Regiment (PIR) inadvertently dropped near Avola, a city of 22,000 Sicilians. Led by some junior officers, this band of American paratroopers became embroiled in street fighting with Italian machine-gunners and snipers during the morning and early afternoon of 10 July. Fortuitously for the Americans, elements of the British 50th Division with Universal Carriers and infantrymen, which had some earlier difficulty landing near Avola, arrived to reduce the Italian positions in the city. *(NARA)*

American military policemen are shown casually leading a smiling group of Italian prisoners-of-war through a street in Vittoria on 13 July 1943, on the way to stockades for internment before transfer back to North Africa. Vittorio was to the north-east of the US 45th Infantry Division beachhead at Scoglitti in the vicinity of the Axis airfield at Comiso. Company G of the 3rd Battalion, 505th Parachute Infantry Regiment (PIR), along with some artillerymen and three guns of the 456th Field Artillery, were the first Allied troops to enter Vittoria. They captured the Italian garrison there along with numerous vehicles and guns. A US Army lieutenant, who was captured by the Italians and held for several hours before the town surrendered, had managed to convince the Italian commander to capitulate, citing that he would be unable to combat the US 45th Infantry Division then landing to the south-west at Scoglitti. This typified the lack of zeal to fight among the Italian coastal defenders. *(USAMHI)*

## Chapter Four

# The Allied Landings and Axis Counter-attacks

The invasion of Sicily commenced at 2330hrs on the night of 9–10 July 1943 with the airborne operations involving elements of two Allied elite, and intensively-trained units, the American 82nd and the British 1st Airborne Divisions. The British had been deployed previously to North Africa after Operation *Torch*, and took part in some parachute assaults during that campaign, earning the laudatory moniker bestowed upon them by the Germans, the 'Red Devils', for the colour of their berets. General Ridgway, after arriving in Casablanca on 10 May 1943, had drilled his division with parachute drops and glider landings near Oudjida, Morocco, as this locale had features similar to their upcoming Sicilian target, before movement to Kairouan, Tunisia, the staging area for Operation *Husky 1*.

The British 1st Airlanding Brigade, under Brigadier Philip H.W. 'Pip' Hicks, was to seize the Ponte Grande Bridge outside Syracuse, Operation *Ladbroke's* main objective. The American mission, Operation *Husky 1*, utilising Colonel Gavin's 505th Parachute Infantry Regiment (PIR) reinforced by the 3rd Battalion of the 504th PIR for a total of 3,400 paratroopers, was supposed to air-drop in front of the upcoming 1st Infantry Division's landing area at Gela in order to protect the vulnerable beachhead from Axis counter-attacks on D-Day by seizing vital road junctions and bridges.

Many factors contributed to the mishaps that were rife for the airborne operations. These included darkness, turbulent winds, a circuitous flight plan, inexperienced transport and glider crews, smoke from the island, and enemy and 'friendly' AA fire, all of which compounded with each other into creating a near disaster hours before the amphibious assaults. The British airborne formations were in complete disarray with many gliders either thrown off course or released too soon causing crashes into the sea. Approximately seventy Waco CG-4A 'Hadrian' and three 'Horsa' gliders crashed into the water resulting in the drowning of hundreds of the British 1st Airborne. The few members of the British 1st Airlanding Brigade who did manage to make it ashore landed in terrain never meant for glider landings as they encountered stone walls or wires resulting in casualties and fatalities. Only a dozen of the over

140 British gliders landed close to the correct place. Instead of a 2,000-man air-landing force to seize the bridge, the main mission of Operation *Ladbroke* was accomplished in a *coup de main* assault on the bridge's Italian defenders by a platoon-sized force comprised of glidermen, glider pilots and sappers. Eventually reinforced to eighty-seven men by dawn on 10 July 1943, the British fought off repeated Italian counter-attacks for seven hours. Finally, the last fifteen men surrendered but were freed within the hour by a British 5th Division patrol advancing north from its landing beaches in the vicinity of Cassibile.

Colonel Gavin's 82nd Airborne's paratroopers too were widely scattered. Gavin had landed 25 miles to the south-east of his intended drop zone. Only 15 per cent of the paratroopers landed near their planned air-drop areas. Fighting in small isolated groups and utilising the combat initiative that had been instilled into them during training, the paratroopers succeeded at harassing Axis patrols, severing communication lines, and on D-Day interfering with enemy counter-attacks toward the Gela amphibious landing area. The American paratroopers protected the exposed right flank of the 1st Infantry Division at Gela by moving on Biscari and fighting along defensive positions on Biazza Ridge, the latter overlooking the important Biscari road and the key Biscari-Gela road junction. At Biazza Ridge, Gavin's paratroopers engaged over 700 infantry and a company of Mk VI 'Tiger' tanks and a supporting artillery battalion of the Hermann Göring Division. A German headquarters report in late July had underscored that the American paratroopers had indeed delayed the Axis counter-attacks following the amphibious assaults in the Gulf of Gela, while inflicting heavy casualties on the Hermann Göring Division.

The invasion armada with its landing assault forces were all staged from the Middle East and North Africa. However, the US 45th and the Canadian 1st Infantry Divisions sailed directly from the United States and Scotland to form the part of the 2,600-vessel armada for Operation *Husky*, under overall command of the Royal Navy's Admiral Sir Andrew B. Cunningham and the US Navy's Vice Admiral H. Kent Hewitt.

The British landing sectors numbered five. In the northern part of the Gulf of Noto was *Acid North*, which would be the British 13th Corps sector and extended from the Cape Murro di Porco in the north to a coastal area almost parallel with the city of Noto. Here, amphibious assaults would be made by the No. 3 British Commandos, the British 5th Infantry Division and the British 50th Infantry Division in the vicinity (from north to south) of Cassibile, Avola and Noto. In the southern portion of the Gulf of Noto were the *Acid South* and *Bark East* landing zones. These would be in the British 30th Corps sector. The British Independent 231st Brigade would land in the *Bark East* zone just to the north of the town of Pachino. Along the tip of the Pachino Peninsula in the Bark *South* zone, the British 51st Highland Division would land. On the western side of the Pachino Peninsula the 1st Canadian Infantry Division,

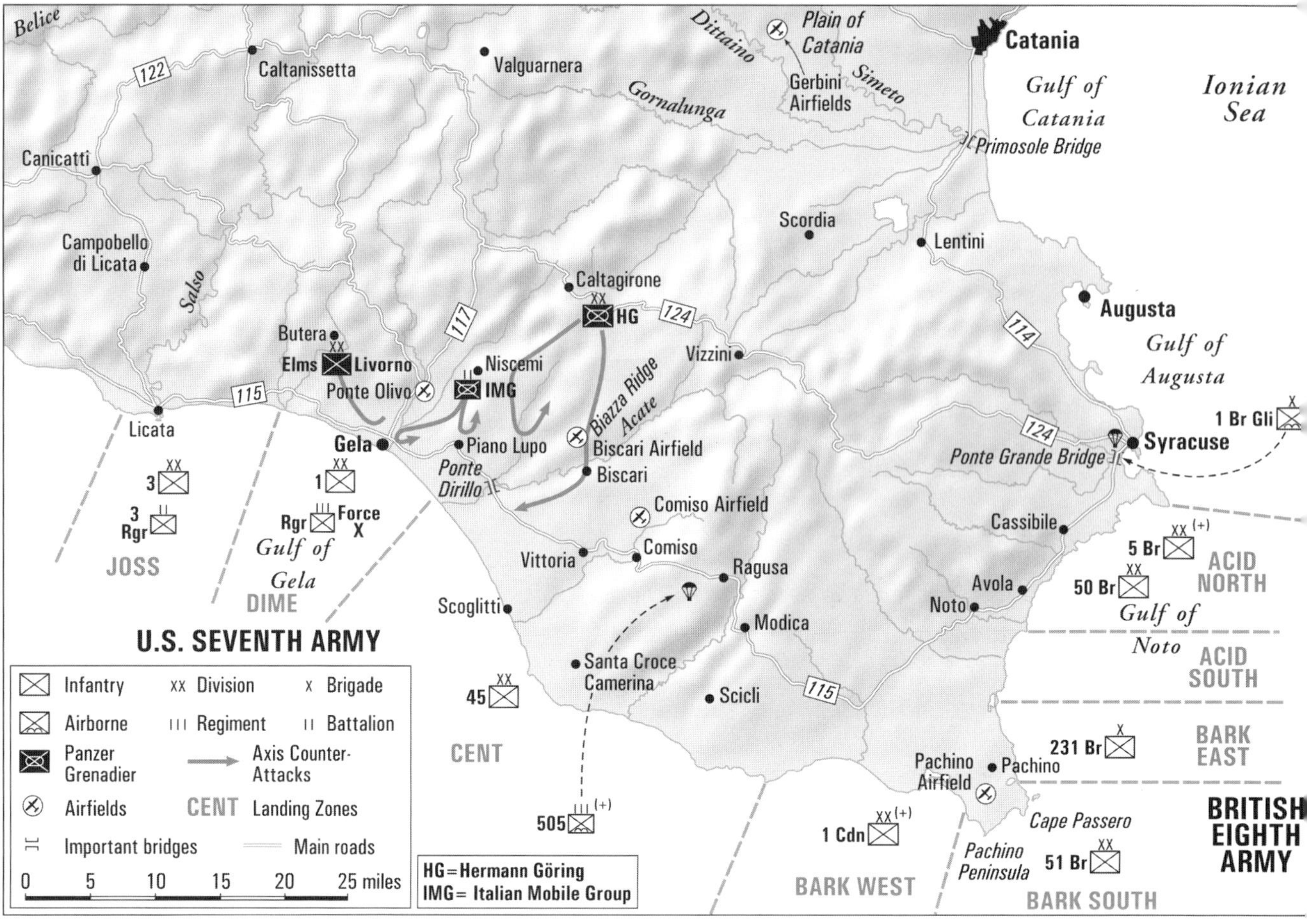


**Allied landings, 10 July 1943.** At 2330hrs on the night of 9–10 July 1943, elements of the American 82nd and the British 1st Airborne Divisions commenced aerial assaults. The British 1st Airlanding Brigade was to seize the Ponte Grande Bridge outside Syracuse (Operation *Ladbroke*). The American mission, *Husky* 1, involved the 505th Parachute Infantry Regiment (PIR) reinforced by the 3rd Battalion of the 504th PIR for a total of 3,400 paratroopers to air-drop in front of the upcoming 1st Infantry Division's landing area at Gela. Mishaps for both missions were rife with troops becoming scattered with heavy casualties incurred. The Ponte Grande Bridge was captured by several British glidermen until relieved by a British 5th Division patrol advancing north from its landing beaches in the vicinity of Cassibile.

The British landing sectors numbered five. In the northern part of the Gulf of Noto was *Acid North*, which would be the British 13th Corps sector and extended from the Cape Murro di Porco in the north to a coastal area almost parallel with the city of Noto. Here, amphibious assaults would be made by the No. 3 British Commandos, the British 5th Division and the British 50th Division in the vicinity (from north to south) of Cassibile, Avola and Noto. In the southern portion of the Gulf of Noto were the *Acid South* and *Bark East* landing zones. These would be in the British 30th Corps sector. The British Independent 231st Brigade would land in the *Bark East* zone just to the north of the town of Pachino. Along the tip of the Pachino Peninsula in the *Bark South* zone, the British 51st Highland Division would land. On the western side of the Pachino Peninsula the 1st Canadian Division, making its combat debut, along with the Nos. 40 and 41 Royal Marine Commandos, would land in the *Bark West* zone. Italian opposition was negligible and the British had yet to make serious contact with

making its combat debut, along with the Nos. 40 and 41 Royal Marine Commandos, would land in the *Bark West* zone.

Opposition to the British Eighth Army's landings was negligible owing to poor equipment, a low quality of training, and an absence of combat morale among the Italian coastal formations that were largely comprised of Sicilian conscripts. The British 50th Infantry Division commander, Major-General Sidney Kirkman, in commenting on the Italian coastal defences stated, 'had enemy resistance on the beaches been at all determined the landings might have well resulted in complete failure with heavy casualties'. By the end of D-Day, the British had yet to make serious contact with German forces. This enabled Montgomery's forces to get firmly ashore and essentially march into Syracuse virtually unopposed, quickly giving the Eighth Army commander an intact port to facilitate his northern movement onto Augusta at the northern end of the Gulf of Augusta.

There were indeed clashes between the British 5th Infantry Division and elements of both the Hermann Göring and 15th Panzergrenadier Divisions, *Group Schmalz*, which was named for its commander, Colonel Wilhelm Schmalz, at Priolo between Syracuse and Augusta. However, the Nazis only slightly retarded the Eighth Army's northern advance off of the beaches. Montgomery's forces would easily capture their objectives in south-eastern Sicily within the initial seventy-two hours of disembarkation. However, the Axis resistance would stiffen considerably as the Plain of Catania was approached.

General Patton's US Seventh Army's assault area in the Gulf of Gela extended from Licata at the western flank to Gela in the centre and in the vicinity of Scoglitti at

---

German forces, enabling Montgomery's forces to march into Syracuse and quickly capture an intact port for the Eighth Army to facilitate further northern movement onto Augusta.

General Patton's US Seventh Army's assault area in the Gulf of Gela extended from Licata at the western flank to Gela in the centre and in the vicinity of Scoglitti at the eastern end. The code-names for these landing forces were (from west-to-east) *Joss*, *Dime* and *Cent*. Licata was attacked from both eastern and western sides by the US 3rd Infantry Division assisted by the 3rd Battalion of US Army Rangers. Combat Command A (CCA) of the US 2nd Armoured Division to provide flank protection of the American beachhead was to also land at Licata. The 2nd Battalion of the US 7th Infantry Regiment of the 3rd Division broke up a poorly-executed Italian counter-attack just over 3 miles to Licata's north-west. US naval gunfire had silenced an Italian railway battery and the port city quickly fell to the 3rd Division. The *Dime* Force, comprised of the US 1st Infantry Division and a regimental-sized *Force X* of the 1st and 4th Battalions of Darby's Rangers, would assault Gela with the task of capturing the Ponte Olivo and Biscari airfields just to the east once the beachhead was secure.

On the extreme right of the American amphibious assault zone, the *Cent* Force was comprised of the US 45th Division. There, near the fishing village of Scoglitti, the pounding surf from the previous night had disrupted the assault infantry's landings. The US 180th Infantry Regiment was scattered along 10 miles of beach. The rocky beach topography wrecked scores of landing craft. Soft sand caused vehicular congestion on the beachhead. The only major combat on the assault beaches to occur on D-Day was in the American centre at the Gela and Scoglitti beachheads. *(Meridian Mapping)*

the eastern end. The code-names for these landing forces were (from west-to-east) *Joss*, *Dime* and *Cent*. Patton would hold in reserve elements of the 2nd Armoured, 82nd Airborne Divisions that were not to be part of the pre-invasion airborne assault, along with the 18th Infantry Regiment of the 1st Division and a battalion of French Moroccan Goumiers.

Licata would be attacked in a pincer assault from both eastern and western sides by the US 3rd Infantry Division of the *Joss* Force, veterans of the Moroccan amphibious attack in November 1942, and would be the easiest of the three landings. Assisting Truscott's 3rd Infantry Division would be the 3rd Battalion of the US Army Rangers under the command of Lieutenant-Colonel William O. Darby. Elements of Combat Command A (CCA) of the US 2nd Armoured Division were to provide flank protection for the American beachhead at Licata. The 2nd Battalion of the US 7th Infantry Regiment of the 3rd Division broke up a poorly-executed Italian counter-attack just over 3 miles to Licata's north-west. US naval gunfire had silenced an Italian railway battery and the port city quickly fell to Truscott's 3rd Division.

Major-General Terry de la Mesa Allen's 'Big Red One' 1st Infantry Division, assisted by the 1st and 4th Ranger Battalions, all comprising the *Dime* Force, would make the assault on Gela and to the east with the mission to capture the Ponte Olivo and Biscari airfields once the beachhead was secure. The only major combat on the assault beaches to occur on D-Day was in the American centre at the Gela and Scoglitti beachheads.

On the extreme right of the American amphibious assault zone, the *Cent* Force was comprised of Major-General Troy Middleton's 45th Infantry Division, an Oklahoma National Guard unit, making its combat debut. There were difficulties in the landing of the US 45th Infantry Division of the *Cent* Force in the vicinity of Scoglitti. The pounding surf from the previous night had disrupted the assault infantry's landings. The US 180th Infantry Regiment was scattered along 10 miles of beach. The beach topography, with its often hidden jagged rocks, offshore sandbars and soft sand ashore created scores of wrecked landing craft in the surf and vehicular congestion on the beachhead, became an inviting target for Axis bombardment from field-guns and aerial attack. Tireless efforts by engineers and beach personnel to lay down metal matting contributed to the movement inland.

## Axis Counter-attacks of 10 and 11 July 1943

*Luftwaffe* General Conrath, in command of the Hermann Göring Division, placed his units on alert at 2200hrs on 9 July 1943 with the advent of the Allied airborne operations. The following morning, on D-Day, 10 July, Kesselring's headquarters in Italy issued an edict that the 'Hermann Göring is ordered to destroy the enemy'. The Italian commander on Sicily, General Guzzoni, instructed both the Livorno Division and two battle-groups of the Herman Göring Division, combined as the

Axis XVI Corps, to stage counter-attacks before the US 1st Infantry Division could consolidate its beachhead at Gela. This response to the Allied invasion was in addition to his moving two Italian mobile airfield defence groups intended for the defence of the Ponte Olivo and Biscari airfields to attack the Gela beachhead. Also, Guzzoni instructed the western elements of the German 15th Panzergrenadier Division, under General Rodt, to move back eastwards towards the centre of Sicily.

Due to faulty communications, made worse by the American paratroopers' destruction of telephone lines, the Hermann Göring Division and the two Italian mobile airfield defence groups struck from the north-east from Niscemi, while in an unco-ordinated manner, a battalion from the Livorno Division headed for the Gela beachhead from the north-west in the vicinity of Butera. Rather than a massive counter-strike against Gela, a series of separate, disjointed attacks were made against the centre of the American beachhead.

General Conrath did not wait for Guzzoni's co-ordinated attack. Instead, he informed General Senger und Etterlin, the German liaison officer to the Sicilian Sixth Army, that he was sending the bulk of his division, that had previously assembled in and around Caltagirone, without delay at 0400hrs, as two task forces, in order to begin his attack by 0900hrs before the sun would be in his troops' eyes five hours later. One of his task forces, an 'infantry-heavy' task force or *Kampfgruppe*, was comprised of a truck-mounted formation of two infantry regiments, an armoured artillery battalion and a company of seventeen Mk VI 'Tiger' tanks with 88mm turret guns. The other task force, a 'tank-heavy' one, had two battalions (approximately ninety) Mk III and Mk IV medium Panzers with 75mm main guns, two armoured artillery battalions and assorted reconnaissance and engineer battalions fighting as an infantry escort for the tanks. Conrath's forces were not as well-trained as the 15th Panzergrenadier Division, and their inexperience caused both confusion and tardiness in getting from the staging areas to the attack points as planned. Conrath's two task forces were intended to be hurled simultaneously at Gela and the junction of the 1st and 45th Infantry Divisions' beachheads, near the mouth of the Acate River.

Thus, during the early morning hours of D-Day, 10 July 1943, three separate Axis forces were on the move: two Italian mobile airfield defence groups (Italian Mobile Force E); a battalion of the Livorno Division; and the two heavily-armoured task forces of the Hermann Göring Division. In an unco-ordinated manner, the Axis units were moving southwards against the centre of Patton's Seventh Army front at the Gela beachhead. The American defence was comprised of: Darby's Force X in the port-city of Gela, the 26th RCT of the 1st Division moving towards the north-south running Highway 117 to the north of Gela's eastern end; and the 16th RCT advancing towards the scattered elements of the 1st Battalion of the 505th PIR, which had set up a blocking position in the vicinity of Piano Lupo, a topographical area comprised of two hills that dominated a road junction where the Gela-Vittoria highway met a smaller road leading to Niscemi and the Ponte Olivo airfield.

The Italian Mobile Force E with captured obsolete French Renault R-35 light tanks, along with motorised artillery had started its movement, independent and ahead of the Hermann Göring Division, in a south-westwardly direction towards Gela from Niscemi on both sides of the Ponte Olivo Airfield. Only a column of approximately ten tanks, without infantry protection, made it into the north-eastern end of the town of Gela and was successfully beaten back by 1st and 4th Battalions of Darby's Rangers, the 1st Battalion of the 39th Combat Engineers Regiment, the 1st Battalion of the 531st Engineer Shore Regiment and 4.2in mortar fire from the 83rd Chemical Battalion. Eventually, elements of the 26th RCT, moving from their assault beaches, made contact with Darby's Force X in Gela and then moved east from the city to cut the north-south Highway 117, and took high ground 2 miles further inland. The other portion of the Italian Mobile Force E, moving south along the eastern side of Ponte Olivo Airfield, would encounter the Americans near Piano Lupo, which Conrath had selected as an intermediary destination for one of his two Panzer task forces.

Concurrent with the southward launch from Niscemi of the Italian Mobile Force E, which was to the west and temporally ahead of Conrath's 'tank-heavy' task force of Mk III and Mk IV Panzers, a battalion of the Livorno Division, considered to be the best Italian fighting force on the island, began advancing towards Gela. As for the Livorno Division's infantry battalion, marching in massed formation, it was decimated by American artillery on the western side of Gela. Not an infantryman from this division made it into Gela and a wide swathe of the fields to the north-west of the coastal town was strewn with Italian corpses and armaments as the remainder of the battalion fled away in panic.

At Casa del Priolo, located between Piano Lupo and Niscemi, a small group of fewer than 100 American paratroopers from the 1st Battalion, 505th PIR disrupted a poorly co-ordinated attack by a column of Italian tanks and infantry of the Italian Mobile Force E. The paratroopers, with only their personal weapons and captured Italian machine-guns, could not effectively oppose Italian artillery-fire. This *ad hoc* American paratrooper force moved on to Piano Lupo, to hopefully make contact with infantrymen of the US 16th Regimental Combat Team (RCT) of the 1st Division advancing from the beachhead and to obtain the support of naval gunfire from US destroyers offshore. A further movement by Italian tanks venturing south of Piano Lupo was stopped by the leading battalions of the 16th RCT and this Axis force retired northwards into the foothills bordering the Plain of Gela to the north-east of the town. Eventually, the paratroopers linked up with forward elements of the 16th RCT at 1100hrs.

German General Conrath's two task forces moved out from Caltagirone after a delay of about five hours and without either providing any mutual support for each other. The 'infantry-heavy' unit with the company of Mk VI 'Tiger' tanks, after crossing the Acate River, approached Biscari, north of the 45th Infantry Division's beachhead, while the other tank-laden force, with about ninety German Mk III and Mk IV medium tanks, and other artillery and infantry units of the Hermann Göring Division, was in the vicinity to the south of Niscemi approaching Piano Lupo and the Plain of Gela at 1400hrs. The two Nazi task forces were therefore making parallel, but independent southwardly attacks down both sides of the Biscari Airfield and the Terrana Creek, the latter emptying into the Acate River.

The soldiers of the 16th RCT with the accompanying paratroopers, who had previously linked up at the Piano Lupo area in the vicinity of Highway 115, gunned down the German infantry, accompanying the medium Mk III and Mk IV Panzers, with small-arms fire from dug-in field entrenchments, sowing confusion among the Nazi tank commanders. Due to the topography of the Plain of Gela, US naval gunfire, with its 5- and 6-inch shells from destroyers and light cruisers, found its mark on the Niscemi Road and disrupted the attacks of the German Mk III and Mk IV tanks. Wrecked enemy Panzers were left on the plain only a few hundred yards from the right flank of the 1st Division's beachhead to the east of the town of Gela, as testimony to the accuracy and pivotal support provided by naval gunfire to break up the Nazi armoured counter-attack.

The 'infantry-heavy' Mk VI 'Tiger' column accompanied by armoured artillery and motorised infantry battalions of the Hermann Göring Division came into contact near Biscari with the 1st Battalion, 180th Infantry Regiment of the 45th Division, under the command of Lieutenant-Colonel William H. Schaefer, along with some paratroopers. Eventually, the infantry, paratroopers and a battery of US field artillery brought the Germans to a halt at 1530hrs; although the dense, terraced terrain of olive groves, mechanical difficulties and the size of the heavy Panzers, and inexperienced junior officers contributed to the lack of manoeuvrability and forward momentum by this Nazi force. General Conrath, via his Chief of Staff, sacked the task force commander after discovering that for no apparent reason one of the two infantry battalions had been held in reserve and that the armour and infantry elements were not co-ordinating properly. A new task force commander was appointed by Conrath's Chief of Staff, and with much urging this unit began moving forward again.

About a dozen of the Mk VI 'Tiger' tanks, in their renewed attack, broke through the 1st Battalion, 180th Infantry Regiment's lines, and many of the American infantrymen along with their commander, Lieutenant-Colonel Schaefer, were captured, while other GIs moved back towards the coastal area in the vicinity of the east-west-running Highway 115. With the 1st Division beaches in the Gela sector now endangered with an exposed right flank between *Green 2* Beach in the *Dime* sector and *Red* Beach in the *Cent* landing area, the timely arrival of the 3rd Battalion, 180th Infantry Regiment of the 45th Division staunched the renewed Nazi attack by the 'Tiger' tanks and infantry of the Hermann Göring Division. The rapid and solid defence by these American infantrymen caused panic among the enemy soldiers, who then fled almost back to Biscari. By occupying and defending the line along Highway 115, the German counter-attacks failed to envelop the right flank of the 1st Infantry Division and drive them back into the sea from their developing yet vulnerable Gela beachhead.

If the Axis forces had delivered a combined, co-ordinated attack, striking the 1st Division's lines at 0900hrs on 10 July as planned by Conrath, the fate of Patton's Seventh Army on D-Day might have been more precarious. Both the unco-ordinated nature and the delay in unleashing the attacks had enabled elements of the 1st and 45th Infantry Divisions to deploy further inland from the beachhead, where they could mount a more formidable defence as had occurred.

On 11 July 1943, a day after the initial landings, General Guzzoni renewed his attack against the still-vulnerable centre of the American zone around Gela, by the remaining armour and infantry of the Hermann Göring and Livorno Divisions, to drive the US 1st and 45th Infantry Divisions from their beachheads. If successful, the Italian commanding general had planned a major counter-offensive against all the British and American beachheads with all of his forces on the island once-combined. Patton countered the threat of a new Axis counter-attack on 11 July by ordering ashore the remaining elements of Major-General Hugh Gaffey's 2nd Armoured Division and the 18th Infantry Regiment of the 1st Division, which was his floating reserve. A planned second 82nd Airborne Division parachute drop to reinforce this area of the Seventh Army's beachhead front had been cancelled for the overnight of 10–11 July, due to the tenuous nature of the American lines ashore.

Kesselring too ordered Conrath, through *Luftwaffe* communication channels, to attack Gela again on the morning of 11 July. Coupled with the renewed Axis ground counter-attacks were to be heavy aerial attacks on the beaches and the offshore transports. The Axis plan was to start the attack at 0600hrs, with the Hermann Göring Division, in three columns, two heavy in Panzers west of the Acate River, and one comprised predominantly as infantry to the waterway's east. One of the tank battalion's would advance via the Ponte Olivo Airfield area while the other Panzer unit would again move down the Niscemi-Piano Lupo Road. The infantry force would renew its attack from south of Biscari and cross the Acate River at Ponte Dirillo to join the two Panzer forces in the vicinity of Piano Lupo. Then, the three of Conrath's columns would converge on the Plain of Gela from the north-east in order to attack the American infantry positions on the beaches and smash the 1st Infantry Division's positions from east to west. The Italian Livorno Division, likewise in three columns, was to move on Gela from the north-west with the remnants of the Italian Mobile Group E in support.

However, Major-General Allen acted first and in a night-time move sent his 26th Infantry Regiment on the left and the 16th on the right towards the Ponte Olivo Airfield and Niscemi, which had been the main objectives of the 'Big Red One' after landing. The 2nd and 3rd Battalions of the 26th Infantry Regiment would be in dug-in positions along the north-south-running Highway 117 by dawn. Again, 1st Division infantry blocking positions would be established at both Casa del Priolo and Abbio Priolo. The Rangers of Force X stiffened their defences in Gela while the battle-weary 180th Infantry Regiment of the 45th Division held a strongpoint along Highway 115 near Ponte Dirillo on the Acate River, with strong artillery support from the 171st Field Artillery Battalion.

General Conrath sent his three columns moving at 0600hrs on 11 July amid an Axis aerial assault on the offshore naval task force. A tactical Allied air umbrella was not present and American infantry requests for air support went unanswered. Support would, again, have to come from offshore US naval warship batteries.

An initial clash occurred as the 3rd Battalion, 26th Infantry Regiment of the 1st Division moved north along Highway 117. Elsewhere, the Italians headed for Gela again, but Darby's Force X and assorted artillery units stopped them. An additional Italian column was sent in by the Livorno Division commanding general from the vicinity of Butera toward Gela, and Darby's troops would have to contend with them using captured Italian artillery and his own 4.2in mortars. Eventually, Darby would receive assistance of 6-inch naval gun salvos from the cruiser USS *Savannah*. The Italians halted and over 400 enemy troops were captured by the Rangers. Over half of this Italian column's soldiers and many of its officers were decimated and lay dead in the field, where they had fallen on the previous day. After these attacks on Gela on 10 and 11 July, the Livorno Division would cease being a combat unit due to its heavy casualties.

After escaping US naval gunfire, German tanks were moving south along the Niscemi-Piano Lupo road as well as from the west after crossing the Plain of Gela. At Abbio Priolo, the 2nd Battalion, 16th Infantry Regiment of the 1st Division confronted the German Mk III and Mk IV tanks at point blank range with all their available weapons at Abbio Priolo. Finally, with the aid of Howitzers from a field artillery battalion, the German tank assault ebbed. But Conrath's Panzers renewed their efforts and the American defenders at Casa del Priolo and Abbio Priolo were compelled to withdraw to Piano Lupo. There, other elements of the 16th Infantry Regiment's battalions managed to hold the road junction at Piano Lupo, even though a handful of German Panzers did manage to break through. However, they were stopped by both the infantry's heavy weapons and paratroopers with bazookas.

Another column of German tanks and infantry moved down from Biscari towards Highway 115 and sent elements of the 180th Infantry Regiment, positioned at Ponte Dirillo on the Acate River, to the rear. This retreat occurred despite the close naval gunfire support of the American destroyer USS *Beatty*, which had fired over 800 5-inch shells at the oncoming Nazi Panzer column.

As the powerful German tank and infantry column, comprised of over 700 infantry of the 1st Panzergrenadier Regiment of the Herman Göring Division, an armoured artillery battalion and a company of Mk VI 'Tiger' tanks, continued to move south towards the 45th Division's beachhead, over 250 paratroopers of Colonel Gavin's 505th PIR, which had previously captured Vittoria, moved in from the east and established hasty defensive works at Biazza Ridge, an area of high ground overlooking the Acate River, the road to Biscari and the Biscari-Gela Road junction. Here the paratroopers and scattered groups of the 180th Infantry Regiment of the 45th Division infantrymen would hold their ground against the stronger enemy forces. Gavin's force was the only one between the Germans and the exposed left flank of the 45th and the vulnerable right flank of the 1st Infantry Divisions.

While attempting to advance westward along Highway 115 in order to seize Ponte Dirillo, Gavin's *ad hoc* force came under fire from four German Mk VI 'Tiger' tanks and Nazi infantry, which stopped the paratroopers' advance. Bazooka rockets, which Gavin was to personally find ineffective against the 'Tiger' tank armour, coupled with the airborne unit's 75mm pack Howitzer rounds and fire from the 179th Infantry Regiment's towed 57mm AT guns, forced the German armour to withdraw after knocking out one of the heavy enemy tanks.

By early evening, six M4A1 'Sherman' medium tanks of the 2nd Armoured Division arrived, along with some Airborne engineers to bolster Gavin's defences against German infantry outflanking moves. A second paratrooper advance on Ponte Dirillo, coupled with the American tanks, came at 2000hrs. A 'Tiger' tank, along with some German 120mm mortars, was captured intact by Lieutenant Harold Swingler, after the Panzer crew was killed. The German initiative waned from the stout American defence at Biazza Ridge and the enemy started to make their way north toward Biscari. As darkness occurred, Gavin organised a strong defensive line and buried his dead on Biazza Ridge. For his gallantry and leadership at this remote Sicilian locale, Gavin would be awarded the DSC.

To Gela's east, General Conrath continued his quest for the American beaches as his lead tanks fired on supply dumps and landing craft from just over a mile away from the sea. What saved the day for the 1st Infantry Division's beachhead was the arrival of the 32nd Field Artillery Battalion arriving in DUKWs and commencing fire at the German tanks as soon as they were positioned along the sand dunes. Additionally, some M4A1 'Sherman' tanks of the 2nd Armoured Division's Combat Command B (CCB) exited the beach to begin firing on the German armour. All 1st Infantry Division personnel formed a last line of defence along the dunes. The combatants were so proximate to one another that the US Navy warships held their fire lest there be 'friendly fire' accidents. However, eventually shells from the cruiser USS *Boise* would begin to rain 6-inch shells on the advancing German Panzers on the Plain of Gela. The German tank column never did cross the coastal Highway 115, and upon their withdrawal were subjected to continued naval gunfire. Over a dozen German tanks were left ablaze on the Plain of Gela.

Unknown to the American defenders atop Biazza Ridge and all along the Seventh Army shoreline front, General Conrath had decided at 1600hrs on 11 July 1943 to call off his second day's counter-attack. He had already lost one-third of his Hermann Göring Division's tank strength. Conrath's staff would later acknowledge in an after-action report that: 'the enemy … is beginning to surround the HG Panzer Division from the west and east … Continued defence in present positions would result in annihilation of the Division.' His armoured units around the Plain of Gela began their withdrawal to the vicinity south of Niscemi and the Hermann Göring Division commanding general would pull his remaining divisional elements back in stages reaching Caltagirone on 13 July.

By the end of D-Day, a 50-mile wide American beachhead across the southern Sicilian coast had been established. The extent of inland advancement varied from 2 to 4 miles with the thinnest area being at Gela, at points where the 82nd Airborne Division's pre-invasion paratrooper drops were inaccurate. Throughout 10 July 1943, over 4,000 Axis (mostly Italian) prisoners had been taken for an approximate American casualty list of under 100 killed, 200 wounded and 700 missing in action. During Operation *Husky's* initial forty-eight hours, 80,000 men, 7,000 vehicles and 900 guns came across the beaches of south-eastern Sicily, in addition to approximately 18,000 tons of ammunition and supplies.

A very unfortunate postscript occurred on the night of 11 July 1943, after the second Axis counter-attack had failed to roll up the 1st Division's beachhead at Gela. More than 140 air transports ferrying Colonel Reuben H. Tucker and the remaining battalions of the reinforced 504th PIR, approximately 2,300 paratroopers, came under intensive Allied naval 'friendly fire' AA gunfire before their intended air-drop on the Plain of Gela. Although given assurances that after following a prescribed flight path that the C-47 transports would not be subjected to 'friendly' AA gunfire, the opposite circumstance happened. US Navy AA gunners were still extremely jittery about the sound of overhead aerial motors, especially since the daytime 11 June massive Axis aerial assault on the fleet off Gela had sunk the American Liberty ship ammunition transport, the USS *Robert Rowan*, which underwent a horrific explosion. Over a score of the paratroopers' transports were shot down and not recovered, while almost forty more were severely damaged, leaving hundreds of paratroopers and aircrews as casualties. Admiral Morison's post-war commentary noted that it was amazingly foolish that the 'Air Force would lay on so hazardous a flight at low level … where enemy raids had been frequent for two days.'

(**Above**) American paratroopers of the US 82nd Airborne Division sitting somewhat apprehensively aboard their C-47 transport *en route* to Sicily from their North African staging area near Kairouan in Tunisia. Prior to that, Ridgway has selected Oudjida, Morocco, as his training site for the attacking elements of the 82nd Airborne since it was a facsimile to the area of Sicily where Gavin's troops were to air-drop on 9–10 July 1943. Practise jumps and glider landings were conducted at Oudjida, resulting in many injuries. *(NARA)*

(**Opposite, above**) US naval warships mounted an impressive anti-aircraft (AA) gunfire barrage at Axis aircraft on the night of 11 July 1943. Enemy fire brought down some of the American C-47s after they had managed to air-drop their paratroopers on 9–10 July. However, on subsequent flights ferrying Colonel Reuben H. Tucker's 504th Regimental Combat Team on the night of 11 July, Allied naval 'friendly fire' riddled and downed several paratrooper-laden air transports. The US Navy warships off Gela, over which the transports were to fly, had been under the largest Axis aerial assault earlier on 11 July, which had unnerved the naval AA gunners. The carnage was devastating as over twenty transports were shot down and never recovered, while almost an additional forty transports were severely damaged. Deaths and wounded among aircrew and pilots alone approached a startling 200 from the 'friendly fire'. *(NARA)*

(**Opposite, below**) A British Waco CG4-A 'Hadrian' glider lying in a Sicilian field after hitting a power line and crash landing during Operation *Ladbroke*, the British 1st Airlanding Brigade's mission. The glidermen's task was to capture the Ponte Grande Bridge over the Anapo River intact to facilitate Montgomery's movement to seize the port of Syracuse. Other gliders also crashed both on land and at sea. *(NARA)*

29

A British Waco CG4-A 'Hadrian' glider is shown as it 'washed up' on the Sicilian shoreline after crashing at sea. The British Airborne's 1st Airlanding Brigade under Brigadier Philip H.W. 'Pip' Hicks were towed from North Africa by C-47 'Dakota' transports embarking from six airfields around Kairouan, Tunisia. The glider pilots were not properly trained in judging distance while over water on their approaches to a coastline. Also, winds and enemy anti-aircraft (AA) fire disrupted the formations of towing transports and their trailing gliders causing some of the C-47 pilot to release their gliders prematurely, which caused them to crash into the sea. *(NARA)*

Elements of the scattered 505th Parachute Infantry Regiment (PIR) that had captured Vittoria on 10 July 1943 are shown regrouping in the town and moving through it in donkey carts and on bicycles. Colonel Gavin had collected over 250 paratroopers in this town just to the north of the US 45th Division's beachhead in the vicinity of Scoglitti. Gavin then moved this *ad hoc* force to the west and, with some scattered soldiers of the 45th Division, would set up hasty defensive works at Biazza Ridge. *(NARA)*.

Paratroopers from Gavin's 505th Parachute Infantry Regiment (PIR) are shown deploying near a treeline at Biazza Ridge, which was atop both the Biscari road and the vital Biscari-Gela road junction, during the morning of 11 July 1943. These American troops had proceeded north-west along Route 115, the Vittoria-Gela road, to meet an enemy counter-attack, composed of infantry and Mk VI 'Tiger' tanks of the 1st Panzergrenadier Regiment of the Hermann Göring Division, trying to get between the flanks of the 1st and 45th Division beachheads. Gavin's anti-tank (AT) weapons included only bazookas and two 75mm pack Howitzers firing directly at the Nazi tanks. Fortunately, by that evening, reinforcements in the form of M4A1 Sherman tanks and some Airborne Engineers arrived. *(USAMHI)*

(**Above**) Paratroopers of the 505th Parachute Infantry Regiment (PIR) are standing behind a German Panzer VI 'Tiger' tank (*left background*) after it was captured at Biazza Ridge. The German Panzer Mk VI 'Tiger' heavy tank entered production in August 1942 and saw action in Tunisia in early 1943. A total of 1,350 were built before production shifted to the 'Tiger II' or 'King Tiger'. Its turret housed the powerful 88mm Kwk 36 gun and it also had a MG 34 machine-gun as well. Due to its complexity, it was difficult to produce in large numbers and its overlapping wheel suspension could become caked with mud and snow to the point of immobilising it. The Mk VI 'Tiger' weighed over 120,000lb and had a limited range of just over 60 miles. Moreover, the steep hills, rugged mountains and narrow Sicilian lanes and roads would hamper this heavy tank's ability to manoeuvre in a counter-attack against the American beachhead. Gavin's bazooka teams on Biazza Ridge had little effect on the heavily armoured company of 'Tiger I' tanks that confronted them. However, Lieutenant Harold Swingler captured this Mk VI intact after he killed the Panzer's crew when they were outside the tank. This German 'Tiger' I heavy tank formation lost over a third of its Mk VI Panzers during the initial three days of combat. *(USAMHI)*

(**Opposite page**) American paratroopers on Biazza Ridge captured a number of heavy weapons from the retreating Hermann Göring Division on 11 July 1943. Shown here is a German 120mm *Granatwerfer* 42 heavy mortar on its mobile base that was seized intact by Gavin's forces after their defence of Biazza Ridge. The term *Granatwerfer* literally meant grenade thrower. It was developed in 1942 in an attempt to give German infantry a close support weapon with a heavier performance than existing mortars to date. It had a circular base plate, a tube and a supporting bipod. Because of its over 600lb weight, a two-wheeled axle, as shown, was used for towing. The axle could then be removed once a firing position was chosen. This mortar could fire a 34lb round over 5,500yds. *(USAMHI)*

SIGNAL CORPS
U.S. ARMY

(**Above**) A British warship is seen firing a salvo at Axis installations on the eastern coast of Sicily on D-Day, 10 July 1943. Unlike other Allied amphibious assaults, the one at Sicily did not have a long preparatory naval bombardment prior to launching the assault waves from their troop transport vessels, as the invasion planners wanted the element of tactical surprise in their favour. However, the invasion fleet was discovered during the afternoon hours of 9 July. The British cruisers HMS *Aurora* and HMS *Penelope* did some diversionary shelling to facilitate the landing operations. *(NARA)*

(**Opposite, above**) A US Navy warship is shown bombarding Axis instillations inland from the landing beaches at Licata, the most western of Patton's Seventy Army's landing areas. Elements of the US 7th Infantry Regiment of the 3rd Division came under Axis artillery-fire there. The American warship essentially was providing counter-battery fire until Truscott's 3rd Division's 10th Field Artillery Battalion landed to support the assaulting infantry against the Italian artillery positions. *(NARA)*

(**Opposite, below**) A British Universal Carrier and a towed gun are shown making it onto the beaches in the Eighth Army sector on the eastern coast of Sicily on D-Day as Landing Ship Tanks (LSTs) and Landing Craft Infantry (LCIs) unload vehicles and infantrymen, respectively, in the background. Along with other ingeniously designed shallow craft such as Landing Craft Tanks (LCTs), Landing Craft Vehicle/Personnel (LCVP) and Landing Craft Mechanised (LCM), the centuries-old problem of moving troops rapidly from ship to shore during amphibious operations was solved. *(AWM)*

L.C.T 355

L.C.T.420

British infantrymen are seen descending from a side ladder on a Landing Craft Infantry (LCI). They had to hold on to a guide-rope to get their footing secure before wading the rest of the way through waist-high water onto an uncontested beach. After having contested some heavy surf, the British 50th Division Infantry commander, Major-General Sidney Kirkman stated that 'had enemy [Italian] resistance on the beaches been at all determined the landings might have well resulted in complete failure with heavy casualties'. *(NARA)*

(**Opposite, above**) British Landing Craft Tanks (LCTs) are shown unloading supplies as the British Eighth Army prepares to fight its way north up Sicily's east coast towards Syracuse and then onto Augusta. The British landings were typically anti-climactic, as the anticipated hard fight on the Eighth Army's beaches was met by ill-equipped and poorly led Italian coastal defenders, who were largely Sicilian conscripts lacking a strong will to fight. These Axis troops displayed only a cursory resistance before either surrendering or fleeing inland. From their experience in North Africa, the Allies had no illusions about the fighting quality of the Nazi formations. *(NARA)*

(**Opposite, below**) A British M3A1 scout car is seen moving down a pontoon ramp into waist-deep water from Landing Craft Tank (LCT)-420 at *Bark South* beach on D-Day. This assault beach was assigned to the British 51st Highland Division of Lieutenant-General Leese's 30th Corps that made its landing on the extreme tip of the Pachino Peninsula. Although the Eighth Army landings, in general, met scant resistance, in contrast to the relatively serene scene above, a more northern landing by the 151st Infantry Brigade of the British 50th Division, part of 13th Corps, at its disembarkation point near Avola, met with wind and heavy seas causing many troops to land on the wrong beaches. *(NARA)*

BM

(**Opposite, above**) Troops of the Seaforth Highlanders of the British 51st Infantry Division casually waded ashore at *Bark South* beach on 10 July 1943. In the background to the left is shown a Landing Craft Infantry (LCI) with side ramps, from which the soldiers descended into the water. The soldier in the extreme foreground nonchalantly smoked a cigarette. *(NARA)*

(**Above**) British stretcher-bearers, in somewhat heavier surf, are being assisted by a guide-rope right up to the shoreline. The British Medical Corps had anticipated roughly 10,000 casualties during the initial week of landings and inland manoeuvring. In actuality, just over 1,500 casualties were incurred. *(NARA)*

(**Opposite, below**) A British beachmaster position is shown in the right background. As the flow of troops and vehicles had accumulated on the beachheads, some matting was laid down by sappers to construct a hastily made roadway to move inland and northwards to Syracuse. With only sparse Italian resistance at the shoreline, the Royal Navy had placed ashore four divisions, an independent 231st Brigade, elements of the Special Air Service (SAS) and Commandos, comprising Montgomery's Eighth Army. The SAS as well as the commando units employed had successfully neutralised the Axis coastal batteries just further to the north of Avola at Cassibile. These elite unit attacks were to be followed by the landings of the British 13th Corps' 5th Infantry Division. *(NARA)*

124

(**Opposite, above**) British troops are seen guarding Italian soldiers who readily surrendered to the Allies rather than tenaciously defend the coastline. Here a line of new prisoners-of-war are marched along the shoreline to board transports to take them back to North African stockades for internment. *(NARA)*

(**Opposite, below**) A British M7 107mm self-propelled artillery (SPA) armoured vehicle called a 'Priest' is shown as it moves up a Sicilian lane from the beachhead on D-Day. The British named the armoured vehicle as such because of its pulpit-shaped machine-gun turret on the front. The chassis was from the American M3 Medium tank and this Howitzer was first utilised in the autumn of 1942 at the Second Battle of El Alamein. This armoured vehicle afforded more protection to the crew of five than its predecessors, which mounted the 105mm on a half-track. *(NARA)*

(**Above**) Troops of the British 51st Highland Division, part of General Leese's 30th Corps, are shown preparing the beachhead at their *Bark South* landing site on the tip of the Pachino Peninsula to receive more infantrymen and vehicles from off-loading Landing Craft Tanks (LCTs). A human chain of British soldiers in the middle of the photograph are seen unloading supplies and ammunition from an LCT. On the western side of the Pachino Peninsula, the Canadian 1st Division landed. From their transports and assault craft, the Canadians were able to see the Axis anti-aircraft (AA) fire against Allied medium bombers that were attacking the Pachino airfield. *(NARA)*

(**Opposite, above**) A panoramic view of the Canadian landing zone *Bark West* on the western side of the Pachino Peninsula. In addition to the vast array of warships, Landing Craft Tanks (LCTs), Landing Ship Tanks (LSTs) and the smaller Landing Craft Mechanised (LCMs) are seen in the background. Canadian sappers worked hard to help clear trucks and other vehicles from areas of soft sand in the foreground. To the left of the foreground, a bulldozer is seen hauling a Canadian truck, which is also being pushed by its crew. Behind it is a long line of Canadian vehicles. *(NARA)*

(**Opposite, below**) Canadian infantrymen filing along from the *Bark West* beach landing zone with Allied ships in the background. To the left a shack is shown that contained an Italian machine-gun position that was captured by Royal Marine Commandos in a hand-grenade attack just moments before to assist elements of the 1st Canadian Infantry Division's inland movement. The Royal Marine Commandos landed prior to the Canadians west of the Ponte Castellazo on the Pachino Peninsula to anchor the extreme left flank of Montgomery's Eighth Army assault. *(NARA)*

(**Above**) A Canadian 1st Infantry Division reconnaissance Jeep is seen as it passes a sign pointing to the Sicilian town of Pachino. This formation, under the command of Major-General Guy G. Simonds, was making its combat debut after sailing from Scotland to join the rest of the invasion armada from the United States and North Africa. Although the Canadians would comprise the left of 30th Corps' beachhead, its primary task was to take the airfield at Pachino. Upon arriving there, the airfield had been cratered by the retreating Italians. However, Canadian sappers and RAF Service Commandos repaired the runway in order to receive Allied fighters to provide tactical air support for the invasion fleet. *(NARA)*

(**Above**) Canadian infantrymen of the Edmonton Regiment are shown marching through Modica to the north-west of their *Bark West* beachhead in an effort to link up at Ragusa with elements of the US 45th Infantry Division, the latter unit forming the extreme right flank of the American amphibious forces landing along the Gulf of Gela. The Canadians reached their Pozzallo-Ispica-Rosolini initial objective line by the end of D-Day +1, and on 12 July, while the British 51st Highland Division advanced and took Palazzolo Acreide, the 1st Canadian Infantry Division cleared Modica to continue their advance onto Ragusa. The aim of British 30th Corps' movement, along with the US 45th Infantry Division's advance off from the beachhead at Scoglitti, was to place a strong Allied force between the Hermann Göring Division and other Axis forces opposing the British 13th Corps north of Syracuse. In this manner, the Nazi force might be prevented from joining the Axis coastal defenders, which had been blocking the road north to Catania along Sicily's eastern coast. *(NARA)*

(**Opposite, above**) An American aboard a US vessel of Major-General Lucian Truscott's *Joss* Force is shown scanning the Licata beachhead and the surrounding inland terrain with his binoculars on D-Day. This proved to be the easiest American landing beach as the Italian 207th Coastal Division put up only token resistance. Landing Ship Tanks (LSTs) and smaller amphibious craft can be seen approaching the beach in the background. There were some rough seas during the early morning hours of 10 July 1943, which both delayed embarkation of the Landing Craft Vehicle/Personnel (LCVP) and caused some unfortunate drowning of assault infantrymen. *(NARA)*

(**Opposite, below**) An Italian machine-gun was positioned in a concrete pillbox at the extreme left of this group of homes, situated behind barbed wire, along the Licata beachhead. The 3rd Infantry Division's plan was to capture Licata from two directions. One of Lieutenant-Colonel Darby's Ranger Battalions was to anchor the landing zone on the western flank at *Green* Beach while troops from Yellow and Blue Beaches, to Licata's east, would function as a pincer moving in on the coastal town from the right. Licata quickly fell once Italian artillery was neutralised by US warship gunfire and landed field artillery. *(NARA)*

386

(**Opposite, above**) American soldiers of the US 3rd Infantry Division moving off a ramp from an Landing Ship Tank (LST) in the *Joss* assault area to reach more shallow water to wade ashore at one of the Licata landing beaches. There were four landing beaches to comprise the pincer movement to capture the port of Licata. These were code-named from west-to-east: *Red*, *Green*, *Yellow* and *Blue*, with the latter two to the east of Licata. At *Red* Beach, the 7th Regimental Combat Team (RCT) landed and received heavy artillery and small-arms fire. While at *Green* Beach, elements of the 15th Infantry Regiment plus Ranger troops arrived with minimal opposition. *Yellow* Beach was assaulted by both tanks and infantry, the former from the 2nd Armoured Division. Only limited opposition to the landing occurred there. The 15th and 30th RCTs landed at *Blue* Beach and moved inland to surround points north of Licata and to form an eastern edge of the *Joss* beachhead. *(USAMHI)*

(**Opposite, below**) Infantrymen are seen individually leading a group of donkeys off a pontoon ramp into the shallow surf at one of the *Joss* landing beaches astride the port of Licata on D-Day. A large Landing Ship Tank can be seen in the right background. Major-General Truscott strongly advocated the shipping of these pack animals for the subsequent 3rd Infantry Division's campaign in the rugged Sicilian hills and mountains. *(USAMHI)*

(**Above**) An American M4A1 'Sherman' medium tank of the 3rd Battalion, 67th Armoured Regiment, 2nd Armoured Division is shown descending a ramp from a pontoon bridge extending from a Landing Ship Tank at *Yellow* Beach, to Licata's east. Both *Yellow* and *Blue* Beaches ran directly parallel to a Sicilian coastal railway line that had some Italian railway-mounted naval artillery that fired on the assault waves but was put out of commission by American naval gunfire. *(NARA)*

196
196
196

The American *Stars and Stripes* (*left*) and the British *Union Jack* (*right*) are shown flying from windows at Licata's City Hall on D-Day. Truscott's landings had captured the port city for Patton's Seventy Army with fewer than 100 casualties on 10 July 1943 to establish the extreme left flank of the American assault. (*NARA*)

(**Opposite, above**) American half-tracks of the 2nd Armoured Division are seen leaving their Landing Craft Mechanised (LCMs) in shallow surf at *Yellow* Beach, to Licata's east, in the *Joss* assault sector on D-Day. The half-track in the centre has two 0.50in-calibre machine-guns, which are mounted for utility in an anti-aircraft (AA) role. (*NARA*)

(**Opposite, below**) An American DUKW amphibious truck is shown off-loading supplies from a Landing Craft Infantry (LCI), with its typical wooden ramp located on either side of the bow, at a Licata beach well after the initial assault. The DUKW was derived from the GMC 6 × 6 truck and had a boat-shaped hull for buoyancy. Over 20,000 of these amphibious trucks were built prior to the war's end. These vehicles were both sturdy and reliable and could transport troops, supplies and light weaponry from offshore to inland positions. (*NARA*)

(**Opposite, above**) At Gela, in the centre of the US Seventh Army's zone of amphibious landings, which was code-named *Dime*, the assault beaches astride both sides of the town were from west-to-east: *Red*, *Green*, *Yellow*, *Blue*, *Red 2* and *Green 2*. Above, wounded American soldiers who had been brought back to one of the beaches atop Jeeps are loaded by litter onto a Landing Craft Mechanised (LCM). The fighting at Gela was much fiercer than at the Licata assault beaches as Patton had envisioned, which was one of the main reasons that he wanted the veteran 1st Infantry Division, under Major-General Terry de la Mesa Allen, to lead the attack there. *(USAMHI)*

(**Opposite, below**) Three Landing Craft Vehicle/Personnel (LCVP) vessels are shown at the shoreline of *Red* Beach, the extreme left of the 1st Infantry Division's assault, on D-Day. A Landing Ship Tank (LST) is seen in the background off-loading troops and vehicles via a pontoon ramp extending from the open bow gates of the vessel. *Red* Beach was assaulted by elements of Darby's Force X of Rangers along with the 26th Regimental Combat Team. *(USAMHI)*

(**Above**) The crew of an American M4A1 'Sherman' tank is seen climbing over the sands at *Red 2* Beach after the initial assault at this Gela beach had been completed, as evidenced by the relaxed posture of the infantrymen walking in the foreground. *(NARA)*

(**Above**) Sicilian inhabitants of Gela are shown going about their business on D-Day +1 as they walk past the wreck of an Italian tank that was destroyed on 10 July 1943, during street fighting between troops of Darby's Force X and an Italian motorised counter-attacking column. The destroyed armoured vehicle was probably a captured French Renault two-man R-35 infantry tank. Elements of the Italian motorised column also took part in resisting the British and Canadian invasion near Pachino on D-Day. *(NARA)*

(**Opposite, above**) An American 37mm anti-tank (AT) gun is shown situated on a Gela street after the town was occupied by the US 1st Infantry Division. Darby's Force X had effectively utilised an antiquated AT gun like this one against the lightly-armoured, outdated Italian counter-attacking tanks of Mobile Group E on the morning of 10 July 1943. *(NARA)*

(**Opposite, below**) Some parts of Gela are shown lying in ruins on 12 July 1943 after the D-Day counter-attacks by an Italian motorised column were beaten back. In addition to anti-tank guns used, the American forces had bazookas and satchel charges filled with explosives. Other damage to the Italian vehicles was caused by accurate US naval gunfire. *(NARA)*

A disabled German Flak 18 88mm anti-aircraft (AA) gun is situated next to a concrete Axis fortification near Gesso near Messina. The legendary 'Eighty Eight' was introduced as the Flak 18 in 1933 and was initially utilised by fascist troops in the Spanish Civil War. The gun's notoriety is based on its dual role as an AA weapon as well as a formidable anti-tank gun in North Africa by Rommel's *Deutsches Afrika Korps* from 1941–1943. Allied tankers harboured tremendous respect for this weapon that was capable of destroying even heavier tanks, such as the British 'Matilda' Infantry ('I') Tank and the M4 Medium 'Sherman' tanks with deadly accuracy. *(USAMHI)*

(**Opposite, above**) An Italian self-propelled artillery (SPA) vehicle, the Semovente 90/53, is shown. Using an M14/41 tank chassis, this mounted 90mm anti-aircraft (AA) gun was a potent Axis tank destroyer and was part of an Italian mechanised unit that fought inland-advancing elements of the US 3rd Infantry Division near Campobello di Licata and Canicatti on 11–12 July 1943. *(NARA)*

(**Opposite, below**) An American supply transport laden with vehicles and ordnance serenely approaches the captured harbour area of Gela. However, on 10 July 1943, German General Conrath had launched a counter-attack against the Gela beachhead with his Hermann Göring Division, independent of the Italian Mobile Group E movement on the town of Gela. Unfortunately, this Nazi formation was neither as well-trained nor well-led as the 15th Panzer-grenadier Division. Nonetheless, Conrath's division was still capable of delivering a potent counter-attack to the vulnerable 1st Infantry Division beachhead, which only had the US Navy's gunfire as its main support in the first days after the invasion. More inland, the small-arms fire of the infantrymen of the 1st Division and *ad hoc* paratrooper groups of the 505th Parachute Infantry Regiment (PIR) of the 82nd Airborne Division contributed greatly to breaking up another arm of the Nazi counter-attack. The elements of the Hermann Göring Division that had attacked Gela possessed truck-mounted infantry regiments, along with a company of seventeen Mk VI 'Tiger' heavy tanks with 88mm turret armament and assorted battalions of Mk III and IV medium tanks with 75mm turret-mounted guns. *(NARA)*

(**Above**) A captured German Focke-Wulf (Fw) 190 fighter and an Italian bomber sit idle on a captured Sicilian airfield during the early part of the invasion. The Fw 190 was more powerful and versatile than its fighter counterpart, the Messerschmitt (Me) 109. However, it was less manoeuvrable and had a slower rate of climb than the latter Nazi aircraft. During the planning phase for Operation *Husky*, Air Chief Marshal (ACM) Tedder was convinced that without the timely capture of the Axis airfields at Gela, 'the entire plan would prove abortive.' The Ponte Olivo airfield was to be captured by the US 1st Infantry Division by daylight on D-Day +1. The Biscari and Comiso airfields, in the US 45th Infantry Division sector, were to be captured by D-Day +2. *(NARA)*

(**Opposite, above**) An American infantryman is seen standing guard over Axis prisoners-of-war, who gaze at the American invasion fleet in the Gulf of Gela. The Italian coastal divisions, which were largely made up of Sicilian conscripts, readily gave up on fighting as they surrendered or fled inland. However, at Gela, a battalion from the Livorno Division, considered to be the best Italian unit on Sicily, was decimated as it advanced in compact formation against American naval gunfire and infantry small-arms, demonstrating its poor leadership. In addition to the prisoners-of-war shown above, American patrols found the bodies and equipment of Italian infantrymen littering the battlefield to the north-west of Gela following the two days of counter-attacks on 10 and 11 July 1943. *(NARA)*

(**Opposite, below**) American soldiers are shown removing a Nazi flag from the Axis General Headquarters in Gela. The sign *PNF* denotes *Partito Nazionale Fascista*. *(NARA)*

P.N.F.

(**Above**) Damaged American landing craft lie beached at the Scoglitti beachhead, comprising the right flank of the US Seventh Army's amphibious assault in the Gulf of Gela. The beaches there from west-to-east were designated *Red*, *Green*, *Yellow*, *Green 2*, *Yellow 2* and *Blue 2*. Two of the three infantry Regimental Combat Team (RCT) from the US 45th Division, the 180th and 179th, landed at their assigned beaches at *Red*, *Green* and *Yellow*. However, a third, the 157th RCT, landed off course to the west with a few landing craft striking rocks near Point Braccetto causing the amphibious vessels to capsize, resulting in the drowning of over a score of heavily-laden infantrymen in the rough waters with 12-foot swells and 6-foot surf at *Green 2*, *Yellow 2* and *Blue 2* beaches. To the right and inland from the 157th RCT were elements of the 505th Parachute Infantry Regiment (PIR) that had become scattered the night before and were forming up on Santo Croce Camerina and Vittoria. *(NARA)*

(**Opposite, above**) Elements from a US 45th Infantry Division assault wave at the Scoglitti landing area, code-named *Cent*, set up a 40mm Bofors anti-aircraft (AA) gun in a nearby sand dune not far from the water's edge where a landing craft can be seen approaching the shoreline. Shown in the background are elements of the US Navy's armada in the eastern end of the Gulf of Gela. All planners of the invasion were appropriately concerned about the imminent danger of Axis aerial attack. *(NARA)*

(**Opposite, below**) A beach patrol infantryman of the US 45th Infantry Division stands alongside an American flag planted in the sand at Scoglitti. Shown in the distance are two Landing Ship Tanks (LSTs), with the one on the right demonstrating a pontoon ramp extending to the shoreline from its opened bow gates. A capsized landing craft can be seen in front of the LST to the left, also with its bow gates opened. This *Cent* sector for the US Seventh Army landing was plagued by submerged rocks and sandbanks that impeded all the amphibious vessels in the assault from making it to the beaches intact. *(NARA)*.

Scoglitti was a small Sicilian fishing village. US Navy destroyers bombarded the Italian defences there with white-phosphorus shells, which terrified the Axis gun-crews in their pillbox batteries. Despite very limited opposition, after the initial landings the American beaches were in total confusion as congestion grew. Above, as the infantry forces reassembled, both on foot and in whatever Jeeps or trucks were available, a column moved through the extremely narrow village lanes to exit Scoglitti into the surrounding Sicilian countryside. (*NARA*)

American soldiers are shown hastily erecting a temporary stockade in Scoglitti for the Italian coastal division soldiers that had surrendered in droves. American casualties had been light. (*NARA*)

American engineers drive stakes into metal matting on *Red* Beach at Gela on 10 July 1943. On D-Day more than 50,000 American troops and 5,000 vehicles landed from Licata to Scoglitti. These engineers were busy preparing to receive the next day's reinforcement waves, tanks and vehicles as well. *(USAMHI)*

US Navy warships and transports in the distance offshore from Gela (*background*). The smaller amphibious vessels at the shoreline were undergoing an intense Axis aerial assault on 11 July 1943. Axis bombs exploded all around the surface vessels as seen from this vantage point above the port of Gela. *(USAMHI)*

(**Above**) A US Coast Guardsman (*centre foreground*) manning his anti-aircraft (AA) gun as bombs are shown exploding in the waters surrounding his transport offshore from the Gela beachheads on 11 July 1943. In the background, both the beach and rising inland Sicilian countryside are visible. *(NARA)*

(**Opposite, above**) An Axis aerial bomb has just exploded in the water to the left of a British transport in the Gulf of Noto while a British warship is shown nearby by with its 'pom-pom' anti-aircraft (AA) gun manned and ready to repel an Axis aerial attack. *(NARA)*

(**Opposite, below**) A Landing Craft Tank (LCT)-153, with its bow ramp down to lower an American troop-laden truck, is targeted by Axis aircraft during the early days of the invasion. The geyser-like splash of a nearby bomb-hit is seen just off to the right of the amphibious vessel in the background. LCT-137 is shown manoeuvring parallel to the shoreline behind the unloading LCT-153. *(USAMHI)*

153
137

(**Opposite, above**) The American Liberty ship USS *Robert Bowen*, carrying ammunition, is seen exploding soon after being hit by an Axis aerial bomb on 11 July 1943. A huge plume of smoke rose up skywards, indicative of the magnitude of the detonation of the explosives on board this cargo ship. *(USAMHI)*

(**Opposite, below**) At Gela on 15 July 1943, a Landing Craft Mechanised (LCM) is seen manoeuvring in the offshore waters to avoid the partially-sunken hulk of an American munitions vessel that was destroyed in the Axis aerial attacks over the preceding days. *(NARA)*

(**Above**) An American soldier is seen inspecting the wreckage of a plane motor that was severed from a destroyed Nazi aircraft just inland from Gela, while in the background, another group of GIs walk to view the remainder of the aircraft and pilot shot down. *(USAMHI)*

(**Above**) Shirtless American soldiers examine the burned corpse of a German pilot with the destroyed aircraft still smouldering in the background. The initial aerial assaults on the American beachheads were temporally coincident with the failed Axis ground counter-attacks on 10–11 July against the vulnerable 1st Division beachhead at Gela by elements of the Hermann Göring Division, the Italian Livorno Division and the Italian Mobile Force E, which were all disrupted by American 5- and 6-inch naval gunfire and US ground forces' infantry weapons and 75mm pack Howitzers. *(NARA)*

(**Opposite, above**) A British infantryman wears an inflatable lifebelt while aboard a transport *en route* for the amphibious invasion reads *A Soldier's Guide to Sicily*. The text probably differed from US War Correspondent Ernie Pyle's appraisal upon landing at Licata. Pyle, who would chronicle the gallant deeds of American servicemen throughout the Sicilian and Italian campaigns, found Sicily to be: 'A drab, light brown country, and there weren't many trees. The fields of grain had been harvested and they were dry and naked and dusty. The villages were pale grey and indistinguishable at a distance from the rest of the country. Water was extremely scarce.' Pyle's prose connoting the image of Sicily is what likely greeted the Allied soldiers, who had become yet another in the centuries-old long line of invading forces to descend upon this often-vanquished island on 10 July 1943. *(NARA)*

(**Opposite, below**) American twin-engine B-25 'Mitchell' medium bombers (*far and top left*) are shown strafing German *Junkers* (*Ju*)-52 transports as they flew at sea level in an attempt to reinforce Sicily after the Allied invasion of 10 July 1943. The Nazis were able to air-drop major elements of their 1st Parachute Division onto the Plain of Catania landing fields, which contributed to the stalling of the Montgomery's Eighth Army's northward movements toward Messina from their initial lodgements in the Gulf of Noto. *(NARA)*

SOLDIER'S GUIDE
TO
SICILY

## Chapter Five

# Allied Advances and Sicilian Objectives Captured

On 12 July 1943, Montgomery proposed a revised plan to Alexander that would allow his Eighth Army to advance north from the landing beaches towards Messina via both sides of Mount Etna. In order to achieve this, Montgomery wanted to move his forces comprising 30th Corps across the boundary, which separated his Eighth Army from Patton's Seventh Army. This modification of the original invasion plan would greatly impact the advance of Middleton's US 45th Infantry Division, the most eastern of the American assault divisions. Major-General Middleton would have to cede the Vizzini-Caltagirone road (Highway 124) to the 1st Canadian Infantry Division of Montgomery's Eighth Army. This 'redeployment' would compel the US 45th Infantry Division to move back to the Gela beaches in order to then move north again to take up new positions on the left flank of the US 1st Infantry Division. This change in road assignment, necessitating the unplanned rearward movement of the 45th Infantry Division, incensed the US II Corps commander, Lieutenant-General Bradley. The Allied 15th Army Group commander, General Alexander, supported Montgomery's altered dispositions and General Patton, in an uncharacteristic docile manner, complied with the Allied ground forces leader. Essentially, these manoeuvres would continue to keep Patton's Seventh Army as a left flank guardian for Eighth Army's northward movement onto Messina.

On the Eighth Army's right flank, moving to the northern end of the Gulf of Augusta, elements of the British 13th Corps completely secured that port-city on 14 July. Now Eighth Army would commence its further movement onto Lentini at the southern edge of the Plain of Catania. The ultimate goal was to capture of the port of Catania and with that the seizure of the Gerbini Airfield complex at the western end of the Plain of Catania. Montgomery's anticipation that Catania would be an easy objective for Dempsey's 13th Corps was short-lived.

As Leese's 30th Corps met limited Axis opposition since its landings, Montgomery's hubris, on 13 July, drove him to make an autonomous decision to send the 1st Canadian and British 51st Highland Infantry Divisions to the north-west in order to move around Mount Etna from that direction to get Messina. Dempsey's

13th Corps would move separately onto the Plain of Catania and beyond. To accomplish this revised strategy, Montgomery, with Alexander's concurrence, usurped Highway 124 towards Caltagirone from Middleton's 45th Infantry Division within Bradley's US II Corps sector for the movement of the 51st Highlanders and Canadians.

With the Eighth Army now divided, the Nazis could quickly dispatch their forces to confront, in detail, each of Montgomery's two separated corps and stop their northward advance onto Messina. Dempsey's 13th Corps had been delayed by *Kampfgruppe* Schmalz in the vicinity of Lentini. The attempted seizure of Primosole Bridge over the Simeto River on 14 July (Operation *Fustian*) by the British 1st Parachute Brigade was initially re-buffed, until its eventual recapture by infantry of the British 50th Infantry Division on 16 July. The anticipated rapid push to Catania became mired down as the Germans established fortified defences north of the bridge on the approaches to Catania. General Hans-Valentin Hube arrived on Sicily from Calabria on 15 July to establish XIV Panzer Corps headquarters on the island and to form an Etna or Hube Line to defend Catania and, ultimately Messina. Hube achieved this with the *Luftwaffe* 1st Parachute and remnants of the Hermann Göring Divisions and some Italian formations.

As Dempsey's 13th Corps' advance northwards to Catania, now stalled by the stiffened Axis resistance, Montgomery ordered him to feign a continued attack towards that port-city to confuse the enemy defenders. Montgomery's main effort would now become his 'left hook' around Mount Etna with 30th Corps, Operation *Hardgate*. Montgomery envisioned that after the anticipated capture of Adrano, a major road junction at the eastern end of Highway 121, by Anglo-Canadian forces during Operation *Hardgate*, the main Axis fortified positions of the Etna or Hube Line at Catania would be evacuated by the enemy, thereby enabling the 13th Corps to resume its advance around the eastern side of Mount Etna against a weakened opposition.

On 18 July 1943, in Bradley's US II Corps sector, Middleton's now-repositioned 45th Infantry Division was tasked to move north onto Termini Imerese and then easterly towards Messina along the northern coast road (Highway 113). Allen's 1st Infantry Division was ordered to capture Enna, which elements of Leese's 30th Corps had instead bypassed on its northward trek from Valguarnera. The seizure of the medieval city of Enna was initially charged to the 1st Canadian Infantry Division, which was not only short of motor transport, but also suffering from the heat and malaria in their combat debut. Also, the city was heavily defended by a German force in the hills surrounding it and the Canadians had run into stiff opposition. Leese ordered the Canadians to bypass Enna to the east, which left US II Corps right flank unprotected. Bradley, the US II Corps commander, informed Leese that the US 1st Infantry Division would capture Enna, which it did in a matter of hours on 20 July.

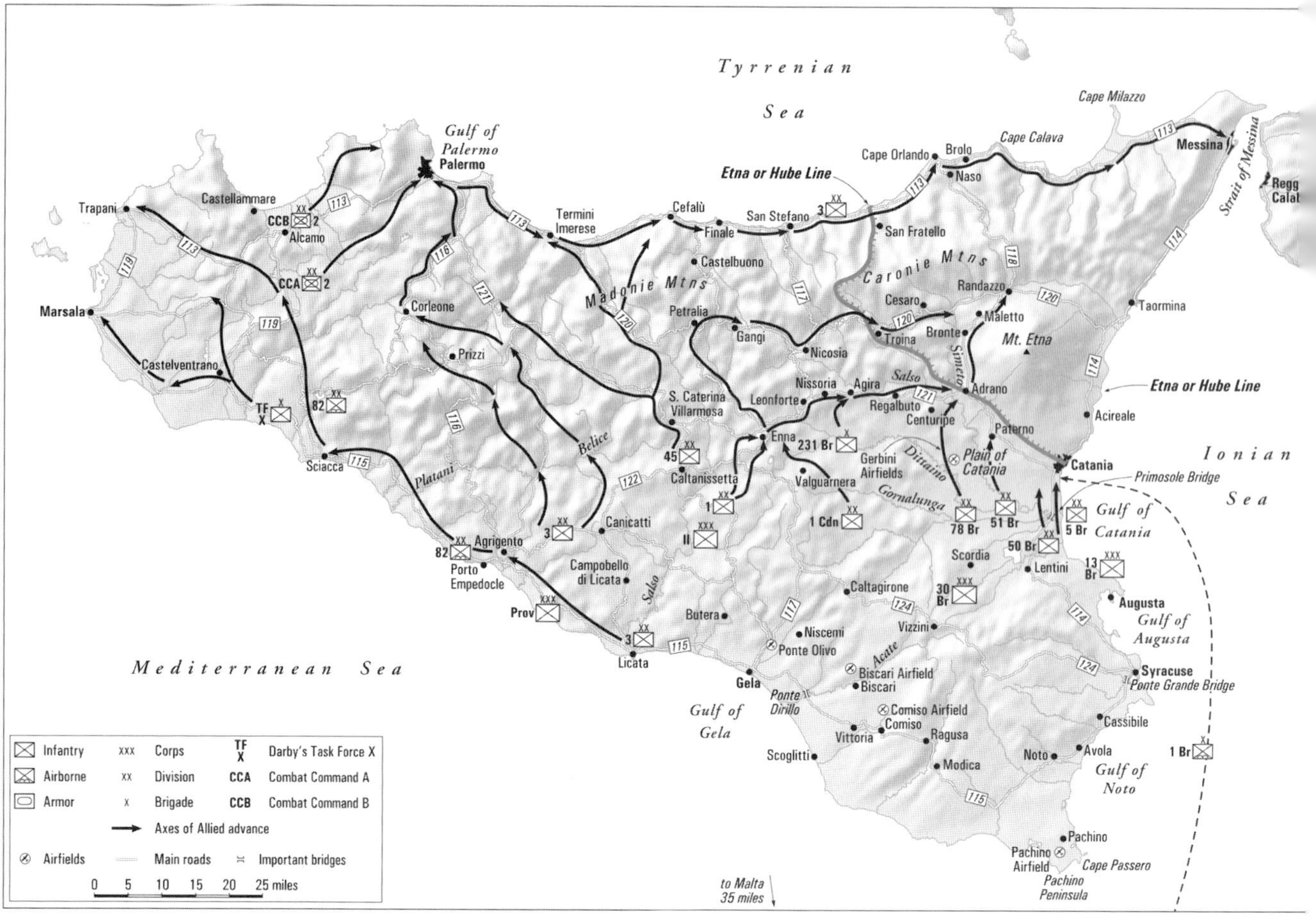


**Allied Offensive thrusts and Sicilian locales seized.** On 12 July 1943, Montgomery unilaterally sent British 30th Corps across Highway 124, a boundary that separated Eighth Army from Patton's Seventh, to allow both of his corps to advance north from the landing beaches towards Messina on either side of Mount Etna. By independently taking Highway 124 for the 1st Canadian Infantry Division, Montgomery compelled the US 45th Infantry Division to return to the Gela beaches prior to a northward move to assume the left flank of the US 1st Infantry Division. The British 13th Corps was delayed by *Kampfgruppe* Schmalz in the vicinity of Lentini, west of Augusta on the south-eastern lip of the Plain of Catania. To hasten his advance, Montgomery audaciously mounted Operation *Fustian* on 14 July, to seize Primosole Bridge over the Simeto River by the British 1st Parachute Brigade. The airborne assault was initially rebuffed until the bridge was recaptured by infantry of the British 50th Division on 16 July. The British 13th Corps' drive then stalled as German defences north of the bridge on the approaches to Catania stiffened. On 18 July, in the US II Corps sector, the now-repositioned 45th Infantry Division was sent to Termini Imerese on Sicily's northern coast with the intent to move easterly toward Messina along Highway 113. The 1st Infantry Division captured the medieval fortress of Enna after the Canadian infantry had bypassed it due to strong Axis resistance. On 19 July, Patton's newly designated Provisional Corps began an initially unauthorised offensive thrust for Palermo and western Sicily. Moving north from Agrigento, the 3rd Infantry Division advanced through central Sicily's mountainous terrain while the 2nd Armoured Division moved from Porto Empedocle to the west of Corleone before turning north-eastwards to capture Palermo, on 22 July, coincident with infantry of the 3rd Division moving to the east of Corleone. Elements of the

The infantry of the US 1st Division then seized Petralia, to the north-west of Enna, on 23 July. After Petralia, Allen's infantrymen were ordered to move east along Highway 120 toward Troina. On this eastward advance, the 'Big Red One' encountered some stubborn enemy opposition while capturing the mountain towns of Gangi and Nicosia, the latter on 28 July, as the 15th Panzergrenadiers withdrew slowly eastwards avoiding a major confrontation with the Americans. Yet to the east was still Troina, a heavily defended mountain town, which led to Randazzo, an important junction, where two roads from Messina converged. Tenaciously defending these mountainous locales in Sicily's central highlands was the 15th Panzergrenadier Division.

Perhaps, as a result of Montgomery's unilateral change in strategy, Patton started to make his own unauthorised operational plans to move on Palermo. On 19 July 1943, Patton's Provisional Corps, under Major-General Geoffrey Keyes, began the offensive thrust for Palermo and western Sicily. Moving north from Agrigento, the 3rd Infantry Division would advance through central Sicily's mountainous terrain, while the 2nd Armoured Division would move from Porto Empedocle to the west of Corleone before turning north-eastwards to arrive at Palermo coincident with

---

82nd Airborne Division moved into north-western Sicily to prevent any Axis forces there from joining the battle to the east. Task Force X, comprised primarily of two Ranger battalions, proceeded from Porto Empedocle along the south-west coast of Sicily towards Marsala on the island's western tip. On 23 July, after Enna's capture, the US 1st Infantry Division seized Petralia to the north-west and then moved east along Highway 120 toward Troina, capturing the mountain towns of Gangi and Nicosia, the latter on 28 July, from the Nazi 15th Panzergrenadiers. The 'Big Red One', reinforced by the 39th Infantry Regiment of the 9th Division, fiercely battled for Troina from 31 July to 5 August 1943. At the end of July, the 45th Infantry Division was relieved by the 3rd Infantry Division as the latter moved east from Palermo toward Messina with a combination of forced marches and amphibious assaults along the arduous, mountainous northern Sicilian coast bordered by the Tyrrhenian Sea. Coincident with the US II Corps movement along Highway 120 to the north, the British 30th Corps commenced Operation *Hardgate* on 24 July, which lasted until 7 August. Canadian soldiers captured Leonforte on 22 July and then, with the assistance of the British 231st Brigade, advanced along Highway 121 through Nissoria-Agira-Regalbuto and onto Adrano, with its important road junction at the south-western face of Mount Etna. Another component of Operation *Hardgate* involved the newly arrived British 78th Infantry Division, which seized Centuripe on 2–3 August and moved onto Adrano. Fulfilling Montgomery's goal, the British 78th Infantry Division, along with elements of the US II Corps, seized Randazzo on 13 August. Messina could now be reached from around the northern face of Mount Etna. The Allied capture of Randazzo compelled the remnants the Etna or Hube Line to withdraw to Messina either northward along Highway 116 to reach the northern coastal road, Highway 113, or eastward via Highway 120, around Mount Etna's northern expanse to reach the eastern coastal road north of Catania. On 4 August, the British 13th Corps resumed its stymied drive northwards up Highway 114 towards Messina. During the evening hours of 16 August, an infantry reconnaissance platoon of Company L of the US 7th Infantry Regiment of the 3rd Division entered Messina coincident with the conclusion of the Axis withdrawal across the Strait of Messina to the Italian mainland. *(Meridian Mapping)*

elements of General Truscott's men moving to the east of Corleone on 22 July. The 82nd Airborne Division's assignment would be to drive into north-western Sicily and neutralise any Axis forces there to prevent them from joining the battle to the east. Colonel Darby's Task Force X, comprised of two Ranger battalions, the 39th Infantry Regiment of the 9th Division (under Colonel 'Paddy' Flint) and some artillery would proceed from Porto Empedocle along the south-west coast of Sicily towards Marsala on the island's western tip.

After Patton's Provisional Corps captured Palermo, and Bradley's US II Corps' 45th Infantry Division reached the northern coastal Highway 113 near Termini Imerese on 23 July, along with the US 1st Infantry Division moving up to its east with hopes of reaching Cefalù on the coastal road, a change in strategy developed. As Leese's British 30th Corps could not open the northern corridor to Randazzo alone, Alexander, at his Allied 15th Army Group command post at Cassibile south of Syracuse, changed the operational objective for Patton's Seventh Army on 24–25 July. Patton would advance towards Messina on two road axes, Highway 113, the northern coastal road with the 3rd Infantry Division, while on Highway 120, the interior mountain road leading from Nicosia to Randazzo, the 1st Infantry Division (Reinforced) would continue on its trek for the bloody encounter at Troina.

General Bradley, the US II Corps commander, in accordance with Alexander's new operational plan for the combined Anglo-American advance to the east, decided on 31 July to relieve Middleton's 45th Infantry Division for the upcoming assault on the Italian mainland at Salerno, Operation *Avalanche*. Truscott's 3rd Infantry Division would now combat the reinforcing German 29th Panzergrenadier Division along the northern coast of Sicily. Major-General Manton Eddy's 9th Infantry Division would pass through the 1st Infantry Division. Since this manoeuvre would take time to assemble the bulk of the 9th Infantry Division, Bradley directed Allen to keep the 'Big Red One' moving towards Cerami and Troina until the Eddy's infantry could effect its relief.

By the fourth week of July, it had become apparent that Montgomery's optimism to capture his objectives on Sicily's eastern coast was incorrect. The 15th Panzergrenadier Division was determined to defend the north-western approaches to Messina above Mount Etna against Leese's 1st Canadian Infantry and British 51st Highland Divisions. Eighth Army's reserve division, the British 78th Infantry, was still in Tunisia and would not be in the battle-line until the very end of the month.

Leese's 30th Corps would commence Operation *Hardgate* on 24 July, which would last until 7 August. Leese's Canadian forces would move from Leonforte, north-east of Enna, which Simonds' infantry captured on 22 July. The 1st Canadian Infantry Division then advanced along an axis on Highway 121, coursing through Nissoria-Agira-Regalbuto and onto Adrano, with its important road junction at the south-western face of Mount Etna that, in theory, once captured would isolate the

Germans in the Plain of Catania. The capture of Adrano on 7 August marked the 1st Canadian Infantry Division's last combat action in Sicily. Simonds' division was pulled out of the line to get prepared for Operation *Baytown*, the invasion of the Italian mainland at the Reggio di Calabria slated to commence on 3 September 1943.

Montgomery hoped that once the British 78th Infantry Division was deployed, Leese's 30th Corps would reach Messina from around the northern face of Mount Etna after seizing Randazzo, which was heavily-defended by the German 15th and elements of the newly-arrived 29th Panzergrenadier Divisions and the remnants of three Italian divisions.

Leese's British brigades of the 78th Infantry Division, once arrived from North Africa, would make the drive for Adrano during Operation *Hardgate* from the south-west through Centuripe (captured on 3 August) and ultimately across the Simeto River to advance on that important road junction on 6–7 August. The British 78th Infantry Division would then continue northwards from Adrano towards Randazzo to execute a link-up with the Americans on 13 August. Before the Allied rendezvous at Randazzo, though, the US 1st Infantry Division, with supporting elements of the 9th Infantry Division, would first have to capture Troina, Sicily's highest elevation city.

The US 1st Infantry Division's battle for Troina from 31 July to 5 August 1943 would be the most costly of the entire campaign and the fiercest since the defence of the Gela beachhead against the 10–11 July Axis counter-attacks. Instead of the Italian forces and elements of the Hermann Göring Division, Allen's troops would still be facing the slowly withdrawing tenacious defence mounted by the entire German 15th Panzergrenadier Division, which was to suffer 1,600 casualties during the Troina resistance. The battle for Troina began on 31 July when the 1st Infantry Division captured Cerami, located 5 miles to the west on Highway 120 across an expansive valley from the mountaintop town, which was now a fortress. Many other hills around Troina also provided redoubts for German mortar and artillery-fire to concentrate on 1st Infantry Division's regiments moving eastward. The 1st Infantry Division was assisted by the 39th Infantry Regiment of the 9th Division and the 4th *Tabor* of Moroccan Goumiers. By the evening of 31 July, 'Paddy' Flint's 39th Infantry secured an enemy hilltop position 2 miles north-east of Cerami. American intelligence estimates of Nazi strength had reported that Troina contained only a few enemy troops and guns, an error that was to play havoc in Allen's deployment of his infantry. Five days of savage fighting comprising American advances and German counter-attacks among the hilltops around Troina ensued with heavy casualties for both combatant sides. There were sixteen US Army artillery battalions of 105mm and 155mm guns supporting the infantry movements. In addition, American A-36 fighter-bombers pounded the German positions in Troina. Another 9th Division regiment, the 60th Infantry, arrived on 4 August, and Allen sent it, along with artillery and engineers to occupy Hill 1536, 6 miles north of Cesarò, to oust German artillery and observation posts supporting Troina. During the night of 5 August, General Rodt's defending 15th Panzergrenadier Division withdrew from Troina to Cesarò, to the east. General Hube did not want Messina to be too vulnerable with his waning troop-strength defending both Troina and Catania and fears that the garrison may be trapped there with a strategic retreat. Elements of the Hermann Göring Division began evacuating Catania on 4 August. On the morning of 6 August, the 1st Infantry Division occupied the ruined central Sicilian city of Troina.

The fall of Adrano and Troina to the British 30th Corps and US II Corps, respectively, compelled German General Hube to commence the logistics for his withdrawal from Sicily via Messina. Adrano had been the anchor of the eastern part of the Etna or Hube Line. Elements of the Hermann Göring Division withdrew from Adrano on the night of 6–7 August and the British 78th Infantry Division entered the city without opposition. Randazzo, the medieval city at the northern base of Mount Etna, was virtually destroyed as it was taken by the British 78th Infantry Division on 13 August, after this formation had encountered strong Axis opposition at both Bronte and then Maletto along the western face of Mount Etna after the fall of Adrano.

The Allied capture of Randazzo sent the remnants of the Etna or Hube Line withdrawing to Messina. Some of the retreating Axis forces used Highway 116 to reach the northern coastal road, Highway 113. Other Axis units moved eastward along Highway 120, around Mount Etna's northern expanse to reach the eastern coastal road, Highway 114, to Catania's north. After the Axis withdrawal from Catania on 4 August, the British 13th Corps too would begin its stymied movement along Highway 114 northwards towards Messina.

After more than five weeks of combat since the D-Day landings on 10 July 1943, a platoon of the US 7th Infantry Regiment of Truscott's 3rd Division entered the outskirts of Messina during the evening hours of 16 August. The following day, General Patton conducted surrender ceremonies in Messina. The Axis had already evacuated Messina for Reggio di Calabria across the Strait of Messina with ferry shuttles in stages, beginning on 11–12 August. The German evacuations during Operation *Lehrgang* would continue through to 16–17 August, when the last elements of the Hermann Göring Panzergrenadier Division were evacuated across the Strait of Messina, which was 2 miles wide at the narrowest point.

An American DUKW is shown as it courses through the ruins of Porto Empedocle on 25 July 1943. On 14 July, Patton told Truscott that he needed to capture the coastal city of Porto Empedocle to the west of Licata, but first needed to capture Agrigento, just to the north-east of the port. Agrigento's capture was needed if Patton's newly-activated Provisional Corps under Major-General Geoffrey Keyes was to have success in extending their advance into western Sicily and ultimately Palermo. Both Agrigento and Porto Empedocle were shelled heavily by US naval warships, principally the cruiser USS *Philadelphia*. By 16 July, Agrigento was captured by elements of Truscott's 3rd Infantry Division while Porto Empedocle was occupied by Darby's Force X. Over 6,000 Italians were captured along with ample military ordnance, including tanks and artillery. Agrigento had a population of 34,000 residents and was perched on a hilltop about 3 miles from the coast and was the gateway to south-western Sicily. *(USAMHI)*

(**Above**) Paratroopers of the 504th Parachute Infantry Regiment (PIR) are shown advancing out of a southern Sicilian coast town to commence their movements westward. On 19 July 1943, Major-General Matthew Ridgway's 82nd Airborne Division, now incorporated into Keyes' Provisional Corps, moved onto Sciacca from their lines to the west of Porto Empedocle. It would be the task of the Airborne to move into western Sicily and neutralise any remaining Axis forces there, thus serving as the left flank for the movements of the US 3rd Infantry and 2nd Armoured Divisions to advance on Palermo. *(Author's Collection)*

(**Opposite, above**) Infantrymen and trucks of the US 3rd Infantry Division are shown moving through the interior of Sicily towards Palermo. This proved to be an arduous task for Truscott's troops since there were still Axis forces north of Agrigento in central Sicily. Also, as is evident above, along the route to Palermo were mountains as high as 4,000ft with narrow, curving roads through them. Along with other elements of the Provisional Corps, the 3rd Infantry Division started their trek for Palermo on 19 July 1943. *(NARA)*

(**Opposite, below**) French Moroccan Goums of the 4th *Tabor* (or regiment) on horseback are seen moving through central Sicily as part of the Provisional Corps on 18 July 1943. The Berber Goumier units all utilised mules as pack animals. Attached to the Goum *Tabor* was a cavalry unit. The terrain shown above was not a hindrance to these horsemen or infantry with their mules. *(USAMHI)*

Elements of the US 2nd Armoured Division, under Major-General Hugh Gaffey, are shown moving down a Palermo street on 22 July 1943 to the cheers of the some of the Sicilian capital's 400,000 residents. It was likely that patrols from both the 3rd Infantry Division and Combat Command A of the 2nd Armoured Division arrived simultaneously in Palermo on 22 July at around 1400hrs. *(NARA)*

(**Opposite, above**) Elements of the 7th Infantry Regiment of the U.S 3rd Division entered Palermo on 22 July 1943. Truscott's infantrymen had advanced over 100 miles in just over three days, mostly on foot. The commanding general of the 3rd Infantry Division had anticipated a need for heightened marching ability while in North Africa. He instilled in his infantry a training regimen to march at a rate of 4 miles per hour rather than the standard 2.5 miles per hour. This marching rate received the moniker the 'Truscott Trot', and many of his battalions were able to march up to 5 miles per hour with full combat kit. Truscott also made effective use of animal transport, in contrast to the Eighth Army, which had had its requested seven companies of pack mules cancelled inexplicably by a staff officer. *(USAMHI)*

(**Opposite, below**) Soldiers of the 45th Infantry Division in Bradley's US II Corps are shown leaving Caltanissetta. Elements of the German 15th Panzergrenadier Division moved from western Sicily to blocking positions in the area of Canicatti-Caltanissetta after the invasion started. Caltanissetta, situated between Canicatti to the south-east and Enna just to the north-east, was an important road junction in central Sicily. Agrigento was 22 miles to the south-west of Canicatti, with the former being the gateway to the south-western coast of Sicily. Highway 122 linked Caltanissetta to Canicatti and Agrigento further to the south-west. It was Truscott's 15th Infantry Regiment, along with armour from the 2nd Armoured Division's Combat Command A (CCA), that captured Canicatti on 12 July 1943. As Truscott had a front of almost 50 miles long, with both of his flanks open, the 3rd Infantry Division commander could not move on Caltanissetta and Enna without reinforcements. Thus, on 16 July, the 45th Infantry Division had to move from the far east of the Seventh Army sector toward Caltanissetta, which fell to his 157th Regimental Combat Team at 1600hrs on 17 July without serious resistance. *(NARA)*

am 20 RICOVERO
am 25 RICOVERO

CALTANISSETTA

(**Opposite page**) Infantrymen of the 1st Division take a brief rest on 5 August 1943 after the bloody five-day battle to take the central Sicilian mountain-top town of Troina. Bradley had referred to it as 'the most bitterly fought battle of the campaign', and it would be the bloodiest for Allen's 'Big Red One' since the Gela counter-attacks of 10–11 July. Troina was positioned at the beginning of the Caronie Mountain chain, which ran almost to Messina merging into Mount Etna. With the Madonie Mountains to the west, this terrain was ideal for a tenacious defender such as the veteran Nazi infantrymen of General Rodt's 15th Panzergrenadier Division. For the German commanders, Troina was to be the northern anchor of the Etna Line. Compounding both the tenacious German defence and the rugged terrain was faulty American intelligence, which underestimated the enemy's strength and desire to hold Troina. *(NARA)*

(**Above**) The crew of an American 155mm M1 Howitzer is shown as it prepares to fire a round on the Randazzo front. This artillery piece was one of a new line of weapons introduced during the early 1940s. With its characteristic split trail, as shown, the crew had only a small protective shield. Over 6,000 of these Howitzers were manufactured by the war's end. The gun could fire a 95lb high explosive shell a maximum range of just over 9 miles. Randazzo was well to the east of Troina on Highway 120 on the northern face of Mount Etna. The 39th Infantry Regiment of the US 9th Division, the 18th Infantry Regiment of the US 1st Division and the British 78th Infantry Division all linked up there on 13 August during the waning days of the campaign. *(NARA)*

An American infantry patrol is shown as it marches through some of the ruins of Randazzo, which was an important road junction that was subjected to intense Allied artillery and aerial bombardment. The British 78th Infantry Division, Montgomery's reserve division that he brought over from North Africa, finally took Randazzo on 13 August 1943 and found the city virtually destroyed. Randazzo was a medieval city that rose from the northern base of Mount Etna. It was the eastern terminus of Highway 120, the interior mountain lateral road that began in Nicosia to the west and ran through central Sicily. Highway 120 was located roughly 15 miles to the south of the coastal Highway 113, the latter running from Palermo to Messina. American and British forces met at Randazzo, which was the road junction connecting the two German flanks. With Randazzo under Allied control, the Germans were compelled to withdraw onto Messina along one of the two coastal roads that converged at Randazzo. It was through Randazzo that the 15th Panzergrenadier Division continued its eastward retreat towards Messina for evacuation to the Italian mainland. *(NARA)*

Soldiers of the General Middleton's 45th Infantry Division are seen inspecting captured German weapons and equipment at Finale on 29 July 1943. After completing their task of cutting the island in half by reaching the northern coastal Highway 113 near Termini Imerese on 23 July, the 45th Infantry Division was shifted east for a drive along the northern coastal Highway 113. Then, Middleton's unit encountered the German 29th Panzergrenadier Division, which had reinforced Sicily after the invasion. For a week, the 45th Division's infantrymen met the fiercest German resistance since its earlier battle for the Biscari Airfield. At Finale, which is located about 7 miles east of Cefalù along the northern coastal Highway 113, one infantry regiment of the 45th Division had to scale steep cliffs in order to evict the German defenders who were tenaciously delaying Bradley's eastward movement. The Germans utilised their mortar, tank and artillery gunfire, coupled with the advantage of the mountainous terrain, to exact a toll on the Americans. Both Patton and Bradley agreed that after three weeks of combat, Middleton's 45th Infantry Division needed a rest. Patton himself praised one of the 45th Division's infantry battalions, 'You are magnificent.' On 31 July, the 45th Infantry Division would be relieved by Truscott's 3rd Infantry Division coming east from Palermo for the final 140-mile northern coastal push onto Messina. The 3rd Division's infantrymen would encounter the same fanatical German defences, 'booby traps', and demolitions that the 45th had. *(NARA)*

(**Above**) An American 4.2in chemical mortar battery is shown firing its shells against German positions at Castel di Tusa on Sicily's northern coast on 10 August 1943. The 3rd Infantry Division's advance against the stout resistance of the German 29th Panzergrenadier Division was punctuated by a series of amphibious assaults in which long-range mortars were needed to support the disembarking infantry when US Navy warships were unavailable. The most costly of these 'end runs' involved a 650-man force of the 2nd Battalion/30th Infantry Regiment of the 3rd Division, under the command of Lieutenant-Colonel Lyle Bernard, whose objective was Mount Cipolla, which overlooked Brolo and controlled the coastal Highway 113. Strong German counter-attacks were beaten off but at a cost of 171 Americans in this force lost. The German 29th Panzergrenadier Division withdrew towards Messina fearing that their avenue of retreat would be blocked after the action at Brolo. *(NARA)*

(**Opposite, above**) Two of the first American reconnaissance Jeeps of the 7th Infantry Regiment of the 3rd Division enter Messina on the evening of 16 August 1943. On the night of 11 August, the Germans began to evacuate the remnants of the 15th Panzergrenadier Division across the Strait of Messina. Truscott's troops were more than 50 miles from Messina at the time. On 15 August, the 29th Panzergrenadier Division started its departure for the Italian mainland. Finally during the dawn hours of 17 August, the last units of the Hermann Göring Division, which had been delaying the advance of the British 50th Infantry Division of 13th Corps, were evacuated from Messina. *(NARA)*

(**Opposite, below**) An infantry reconnaissance platoon of Company L of the US 7th Infantry Regiment of the 3rd Division is seen cautiously moving down a Messina street wary of enemy snipers during the evening hours of 16 August. Other American infantry units arrived on the morning of 17 August. British Commandos, accompanied by some British 'Sherman' tanks, also entered Messina on the morning of 17 August. *(NARA)*

MESSINA

(**Opposite, above**) A Canadian soldier is shown as he stands over the wreck of a German tank in Leonforte on 22 July 1943. This town along the western corridor of Highway 121 was supposed to be captured by the Canadians by the night of 19 July. However, it was ably defended by a Panzergrenadier regiment, the 104th, of the German 15th Panzergrenadier Division. Canadian brigades of the 1st Canadian Infantry Division faced very strong Nazi resistance at both Leonforte and at Assoro, a central Sicilian town to the south-east, which dominated the valley leading to Leonforte. However, in a night-time *coup de main* assault up the face of mountain on 20–21 July, a force of Canadian volunteers surprised the German defenders and captured Assoro without any casualties. Their new position commanded the entire valley below and this force, from the Hastings and Prince Edward Regiment, successfully beat off Nazi counter-attacks. With Assoro captured, the Canadians were able to overcome the stubborn German resistance at Leonforte by 22 July. The Canadians incurred almost 300 casualties in these engagements, with the most occurring in Leonforte. *(NARA)*

(**Opposite, below**) Canadian sappers inspect a destroyed German tracked vehicle for salvage at Nissoria during the start of Operation *Hardgate* on 24 July 1943 along the Highway 121 corridor towards Adrano at the south-western base of Mount Etna. Both combatant sides would attempt to remove disabled armoured vehicles from the battlefield, the Germans using them to bolster their makeshift defensive positions. *(NARA)*

(**Above**) A British patrol from the 17th Infantry Brigade is shown as it passes through a heavily shelled section of Augusta, which fell to the British within days after the invasion. On 12 July 1943, the Italian port city's defenders had destroyed their naval guns and fuel stores and then fled north to Catania as they feared a seaborne invasion. On that day, a Special Air Service (SAS) Reconnaissance Squadron was landed in Augusta Harbour accompanied by three Royal Navy destroyers. By late evening of 12 July, the SAS force found the port largely deserted as columns of the British 17th Infantry Brigade (comprised of elements of the Royal Scots Fusiliers, Northamptonshire Regiment, and the Seaforth Highlanders) of the British 5th Division entered the city. *(NARA)*

(**Opposite page**) A British patrol from the 38th Infantry Brigade of the 78th Division, deployed now as Montgomery's reserve from Tunisia, is shown searching for Axis snipers in the hill town of Centuripe on 3 August 1943, during Operation *Hardgate*. The capture of Centuripe would enable the 78th Infantry Division to continue its north-western movement across the Salso and Simeto Rivers onto the important road junction town of Adrano. *(NARA)*

(**Above**) British soldiers of the 78th Infantry Division, which was attached to Leese's 30th Corps after their arrival from Tunisia, are seen advancing through the ruins of Adrano on the night of 6–7 August. At the instigation of the 30th Corps commander, Adrano was levelled by Allied bombers. On the trek of these infantrymen from the 36th Brigade, as part of Operation *Hardgate*, they pass the corpse of an Italian soldier (*left, foreground*). The town was also heavily defended by elements of the Hermann Göring Division. The capture of Adrano would secure the northern approaches to Messina around the western face of Mount Etna toward Randazzo. This operation was concurrent with British 13th Corps holding the eastern flank on the Plain of Catania. German General Hube had also tightened his defences along the Etna or Hube Line, which ran from Catania to Adrano, and then north-west to Troina and finally to the northern coast. The fall of Adrano, as well as Troina to the US 1st Infantry Division, compelled Hube to initiate the final withdrawal from Sicily. *(NARA)*

British soldiers of the 9th Durham Light Infantry, on 8 August 1943, are seen setting up a temporary Bren gun covering position along the Via Vittorio Emannuelle in the coastal town of Acireale, 10 miles to the north of Catania at the foot of Mount Etna on Sicily's eastern coast facing the Ionian Sea. It took the British 50th Infantry Division two days to capture the town and reduce the defensive roadblocks established by Axis forces. *(NARA)*

(**Opposite, above**) British mechanised troops of the 17th Infantry Brigade of the British 5th Division, a part of Dempsey's 13th Corps, are shown sitting atop a Canadian-built Otter armoured car in the town of Misterbianco on the outskirts of Catania on 5 August 1943. There, they were mobbed by cheering Sicilian residents. Montgomery had earlier hoped to reach Misterbianco on 20 July. However, his attacks by the 5th and 50th Infantry Divisions of British 13th Corps met heavy German resistance and, thus, made limited progress. On the night of 19 July, the British 15th Infantry Brigade of the 5th Division tried to enlarge a foothold across the Simeto River north of the Primosole Bridge and seize Misterbianco. However, during the ensuing twenty-four-hour engagement, the regimental elements in this formation took heavy casualties from German artillery-fire, forcing them to withdraw under their own artillery umbrella, thus leaving Misterbianco in Axis hands. It was not until the fall of Troina and Adrano that German resistance slackened, enabling Dempsey's troops to reach the suburbs of Catania. *(NARA)*

(**Opposite, below**) A British Universal Carrier is seen leading a mechanised procession through the throngs of cheering Sicilians lined-up along a street in Catania. The seizure of this Sicilian city was the key to the strategic capture of Messina. Although Montgomery had showed boldness in his nocturnal airborne attack to seize Primosole Bridge across the Simeto River on 13–14 July, just 5 miles from Catania, the ensuing tardiness to pursue his attack against the retreating Axis forces trying to retain their positions around the bridge, showed too much of his tendency towards conservatism in pursuit of the enemy. In hindsight, some have argued that a co-ordinated ground, sea and aerial assault on Catania, soon after the seizure of the Primosole Bridge, would have compelled Catania's German defends to withdraw further north towards Mount Etna. *(NARA)*

A trio of the East Yorks are shown manning a British Bren gun position with the Italian mainland directly across the Strait of Messina from them one week after Montgomery's Eighth Army marched into Messina. The invasion of Reggio di Calabria by Montgomery's troops would soon commence. *(NARA)*

# Epilogue

The Sicilian campaign did present opportunities to the Allies to achieve an early decisive victory without committing two of its armies to confront the Axis forces in a thirty-eight-day battle of attrition. The greatest opportunity for the Allies was to prevent the Axis forces from either evacuating or being reinforced via the Strait of Messina. Rather than neutralising the port of Messina after the successful landings on eastern and south-eastern Sicily, the Allies instead chose to confront an Italian-German force, never comprised of more than 60,000 Nazis, in horrific mountainous terrain and towns for the mechanised US Seventh and British Eighth Armies to campaign in. By perhaps not seizing Calabria on the Italian mainland across the Strait of Messina early after the amphibious landings of 10 July 1943, the Allies were unable to place the 'cork in the bottle'. This post-battle commentary has remained a lingering controversy about the tardy Allied Sicilian campaign victory.

The overall German commander for the southern front, General Kesselring, commenting upon the invasion's strategy stated that had the Allies mounted a 'secondary attack on Calabria [it] would have enabled the Sicily landing to be developed into a devastating victory'. Other German commanders were also baffled by the Allies' costly mistake to not have attempted an invasion of Calabria prior to the end of the Sicilian campaign. General Heinrich von Vietinghoff, who was to command the German Tenth Army in its defence of southern Italy, in commenting about Calabria's seizure before the Axis evacuation, 'On both sides of the Straits … this would have been possible without any special difficulty.'

The Germans began to oversee the evacuation plan from Sicily to the 'toe of Italy' via the Strait of Messina, Operation *Lehrgang* ('Instruction Course'), in late July 1943. The Strait's ferrying operation would be protected by hundreds of both anti-aircraft (AA) guns and coastal batteries in both Messina and Reggio di Calabria from Allied air-raids, which commenced on 1 August and continued up until 17 August. About 70,000 Italians and 40,000 Germans were evacuated with close to fifty Nazi tanks and almost 200 Axis artillery pieces.

Operation *Baytown*, launched 3 September 1943, saw elements of Montgomery's XIIIth Corps crossed the Strait of Messina to Reggio di Calabria with minimal opposition, following RAF bombing sorties and an artillery barrage from both Allied guns lining the Sicilian shoreline and Royal Navy battleships. Montgomery's Chief of Staff, Brigadier Francis 'Freddie' de Guingand, quipped about the landing's enormous aerial, artillery and naval support, that it was like taking 'a sledgehammer to crack a nut'.

The fascist leaders in Rome had voted on 24 July 1943 against Mussolini's continued stay in power. A week later, Italian King Victor Emmanuel approved a secret emissary going to Portugal to discuss an armistice with the British and Americans. It would still require weeks of clandestine diplomatic negotiations to solidify an armistice agreement. It was not until 3 September, meeting in secret, that Eisenhower and British and American members of the Allied Forces Headquarters, signed an armistice with Italian representatives. In the meantime, Hitler had been in the process of planning to seize control of Italy with *Wehrmacht* troops, if an Italian surrender fractured the Axis alliance. The armistice was officially announced on 8 September. The next day, Lieutenant-General Mark W. Clark's Anglo-American Fifth Army of more than 80,000 troops would assault the beaches along the Gulf of Salerno, south of Naples, to commence Operation *Avalanche*. This invasion of the Italian mainland was to be contested ferociously by the German occupiers leading to what would be one of the fiercest and often forgotten campaigns of the Second World War, the Allied campaign in Italy.

Many of the main objectives of the invasion of Sicily had been completed. With the conquest of Sicily, the Mediterranean Sea had been completely open to the Allies from Axis interdiction. Secondly, fascist Italy had been 'knocked out' of the war. Thirdly, with the sudden loss of Italian divisions from the Axis defences, the southern flank of Hitler's Fortress Europe had to be reinforced by shifting *Wehrmacht* forces from the Russian Front to the southern Mediterranean theatre. In fact, Hitler had halted his Kursk offensive on 13 July 1943, in part due to suspicion of an Italian withdrawal from the Axis alliance should Sicily be lost to the Allies. Fourthly, Allied cohesion at mounting amphibious landings and conducting campaigns via primarily naval lines of communication continued to improve as the daunting task of invading north-west Europe still loomed as the major goal of the US Army command and planners.

However, as to not under-appreciate the cost in human life (i.e. the 'grim butcher's bill') for achieving these objectives, the US Seventh Army lost over 2,200 troops killed and over 5,900 wounded. Their Eighth Army comrades suffered just over 2,000 troops killed and over 7,100 wounded. The US Navy and Royal Navy suffered a combined 860 sailors killed and 895 wounded. The campaign's losses were severe for the Italian defenders on Sicily. There were almost 4,700 killed and another 5,000 wounded with over 150,000 missing or captured. German losses during the Sicilian campaign were over each 4,500 killed and missing. Over 5,000 Germans were captured while an additional 13,500 were wounded and had to be evacuated to the Italian mainland. These figures do not touch upon the large number of casualties among the civilian population during the pre-assault bombardment of the island and intense combat during this thirty-eight-day campaign following the invasion of Sicily.

A bullet-ridden portrait of *Il Duce*, the Italian fascist leader Benito Mussolini, is shown hanging defaced and askew from a wooden telephone pole on Sicily. The Fascist Grand Council in Rome met on 24 July 1943 and voted against Mussolini's continued stay in power. The next day, in an audience with the Italian King Victor Emmanuel, the monarch insisted that Mussolini resign as Marshal Pietro Badoglio had already been selected as his replacement. (*NARA*)

(**Above**) With the Axis evacuation and Allied entry into Messina, two vestiges of the enemy are shown above. In the foreground was a wrecked German troop-carrying tractor lying upside down in a crater at Messina's waterfront. In the middle portion of the photograph was a beached Italian merchant ship that was scuttled after one of the numerous Allied air-raids on this port city to interdict the Axis evacuation of its armed forces from Sicily. Finally, in the background, the Italian mainland is shown. Its proximity is clearly demonstrated across the 2-mile wide Strait of Messina, which took about thirty minutes for a ferry barge evacuating troops and *matériel* to cross. *(NARA)*

(**Opposite, above**) The main signatories of an Italian armistice are shown meeting on 3 September 1943 in secret to execute the document. From left-to-right are: Major-General Walter Bedell Smith (*seated*), General Eisenhower's Chief of Staff; Commodore Reyer Mylions Dick, Royal Navy; Major-General Lowell Rocks, US Army; Captain de Hand, an *aide-de-camp* to Brigadier Kenneth Strong, British Army; and Eisenhower's chief intelligence officer (*who is seen standing to the right*); Italian Lieutenant-General Aldo Castilland (*in mufti*); Mr Montenari, an emissary from the Italian Foreign Ministry (*far right*). The armistice was officially announced on 8 September. *(NARA)*

(**Opposite, below**) An Italian Navy warship that had escaped from the mainland after the armistice is shown sailing into Palermo Harbor on 12 September 1943, four days after the armistice was officially announced. In addition to Italian naval assets joining the Allied coalition, over eighty Italian Army divisions scattered across the Balkans and in Russia would no longer be belligerents for the Axis. *(NARA)*

183172

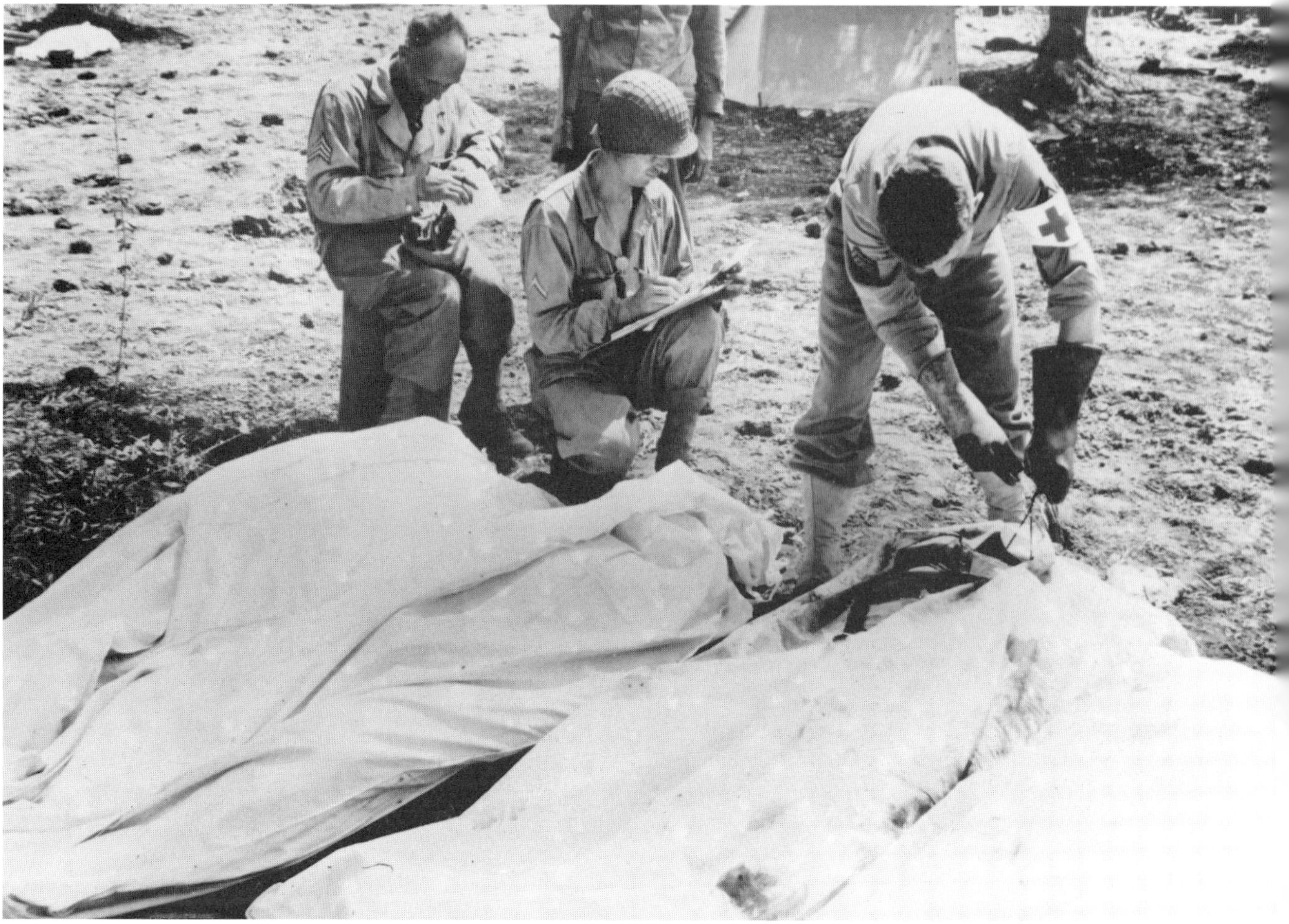

A US Army Medical Corps sergeant is shown removing the dog tags that identify a deceased soldier before burial by the Graves Registration Unit. The soldier was with the US 3rd Infantry Division when he was killed in the San Fratello area just south of Sicily's northern coast in the foothills of the Caronie Mountains. *(NARA)*.

A temporary burial site for one of the first American servicemen, a sailor, killed at Gela on 10 July 1943. His name and military identification number are handwritten on the wooden cross. Many of the casualties among the seamen were incurred in the heavy Axis aerial assaults on the various invasion flotillas off-shore from the landing sectors. *(NARA)*

Two Italian prisoners-of-war, now gravediggers, are shown standing by with their shovels in the foreground as US Army Chaplain Lloyd E. Langford conducts a burial service for the recently interred dead US 3rd Division infantrymen at the San Fratello cemetery on Sicily's northern coast. *(NARA)*

Two Canadian officers are seen inspecting the makeshift grave of a deceased Italian soldier identified by his rifle and cap on a small wooden cross while another soldier examined an abandoned Italian artillery piece. *(NARA)*

A temporary German soldier's grave was marked by his battle helmet perched atop a wooden stake in front of a disabled Nazi Mk IV Panzer. The German Panzergrenadier divisions during the Sicilian campaign lost 170 tanks, which represented about 80 per cent of their armoured strength on the island. Only forty-seven German Panzers were ferried from Messina to the Italian mainland. *(NARA)*

(**Above**) An American 155mm 'Long Tom' cannon crew is shown as they cover their ears to fire a shell across the Strait of Messina at Axis positions. This bombardment of Reggio di Calabria was in preparation for Montgomery's crossing of the Strait of Messina, Operation *Baytown*, on 3 September 1943. On 9 September, Allied forces under Lieutenant-General Mark W. Clark, would undertake Operation *Avalanche*, the amphibious assault on the beaches of the Gulf of Salerno to the south of Naples. *(NARA)*

(**Opposite, above**) Operation *Baytown*, the crossing of the Strait of Messina by British XIII Corps to seize Reggio di Calabria, commenced on 3 September as DUKWs with British infantry departed from the north-eastern Sicilian shoreline for the 'toe of Italy' on the Italian mainland. The crossing and landing at Reggio di Calabria was quite easy as elements of the Canadian 1st and British 5th Infantry Divisions were accompanied by an armoured brigade, British commandos and the 1st Special Raiding Squadron of the Special Air Service. *(USAMHI)*

(**Opposite, below**) Montgomery salutes British infantrymen of XIII Corps as they march through Reggio di Calabria after crossing the Strait of Messina during Operation *Baytown*. These soldiers, although appearing cheerful in this photograph, had experienced the extreme difficulties of the Sicilian campaign, which were even more gruelling than the protracted 'see-saw' battles of the Western Desert, and then the post-Alamein pursuit of Rommel and defeat of the Axis forces in south-eastern Tunisia. *(NARA)*

C29

# References


**Atkinson**, Rick. *The Day of Battle. The War in Sicily and Italy, 1943–1944.* Holt Paperbacks, New York, 2007.

**Blumenson**, Martin. *Sicily. Whose Victory?* Ballentine Books, New York, 1969.

**D'Este**, Carlo. *Bitter Victory. The Battle for Sicily, 1943.* Harper Perennial, New York, 1988.

**D'Este**, Carlo. *World War II in the Mediterranean 1942–1945.* Algonquin Books, Chapel Hill, 1990.

**Diamond**, Jon. *First Blood in North Africa: Operation Torch and the US Campaign in Africa in WWII.* Stackpole Books, Mechanicsburg, 2017.

**Garland**, Albert N. and **Smyth**, Howard M. *The Mediterranean Theater of Operations. Sicily and the Surrender of Italy.* United States Army in World War II. Center of Military History, Washington, DC, 1965.

**Henry**, Mark R. *The US Army in World War II (2). The Mediterranean.* Osprey Publishing, Oxford, 2000.

**Neillands**, Robin. *Eighth Army: The Triumphant Desert Army That Held the Axis at Bay from North Africa to the Alps, 1939–45.* Overlook Press, Woodstock, 2004.

**Perret**, Geoffrey. *There's A War to be Won. The United States Army in World War II.* Ballentine Books, New York, 1991.

**Porch**, Douglas. *The Path to Victory. The Mediterranean Theater in World War II.* Farrar, Straus and Giroux, New York, 2004.

**Tucker-Jones**, Anthony. *Armoured Warfare in the Italian Campaign 1943–1945.* Pen & Sword, Barnsley, 2013.

**Whiting**, Charles. *Slaughter Over Sicily.* Pen & Sword, Barnsley, 1992.

**Zaloga**, Steven J. *Sicily 1943. The Debut of Allied Joint Operations.* Osprey Publishing, Oxford, 2013.

**Zuehlke**, Mark. *Operation Husky. The Canadian Invasion of Sicily, July 10–August 7, 1943.* Douglas & McIntyre, Vancouver, 2010.